MW00629214

The Bible Book by Book

The Bible Book by Book

by

J. B. TIDWELL, A.M., D.D., LL.D.

Professor of Biblical Literature
Baylor University
Waco, Texas

WM. B. EERDMANS PUBLISHING CO.
Grand Rapids Michigan

Reprinted, April 1983

PHOTOLITHOPRINTED BY EERDMANS PRINTING COMPANY
GRAND RAPIDS, MICHIGAN, UNITED STATES OF AMERICA

DEDICATED

TO

THE THOUSANDS OF STUDENTS
THE AUTHOR HAS TAUGHT
DURING THE YEARS

•

Preface

•

THIS ninth edition of "The Bible Book by Book" goes forth with the author's profound gratitude for the reception it has had and with his earnest prayer that it may be more helpful than former editions have been. Certain changes have been made in the hope that it may be more usable and useful. These changes are indicated here.

1. **General Corrections.** All the material, including Scripture references, has been carefully corrected. All the conclusions have been verified and given a statement that it is in accordance with the sanest and most spiritual understanding of the divine books.

2. **Introductory Chapters.** The introductory studies were found to contain much that was repeated in the discussions and topics for study on the several books. This material has, therefore, been omitted and other studies, that seem to be of more general importance, inserted.

3. **Messages of the Books.** The lessons or messages of the several books, which were given in the first edition and omitted in the second, have, with a few changes, been re-inserted here. Experience indicates that they give the student a certain zest in study and discussion and that they leave with him a lasting impression of the importance of each book. These teachings or messages are given in connection with the Old Testament books, but none are given based on the books of the New Testament, since these books seem themselves to be messages.

4. **Scheme of Lessons.** To meet the need of some teachers in trying to cover the entire book, a scheme of lessons has been provided. The assignments are indicated at the beginning of each chapter and are numbered continuously to the end. A margin is left to allow for the study of the introductory chapters, for holidays, for occasional tests, and for examination, and still to enable a class reciting five times a week for a school session of nine months to complete the book. It is hoped that this feature will make the book

more definitely suited for use in our academies and secondary schools without in the least affecting its value to other classes of students.

From the first the aim of the book has been to furnish Bible students with an outline of study which will enable them to gain a certain familiarity with it contents. It is intended especially for students in academies and secondary schools and for certain types of college students. It has also been planned to meet the needs of classes conducted by women's societies, young people's organizations and advanced Sunday school classes, as well as to provide Christians in general with a book that will give them some insight into the purpose, occasion and general setting of each book of the Bible.

The work has been done with a conviction that a knowledge of Christianity and of the simple facts of the history, geography and chronology of the Bible are essential to a liberal education, and that to be familiar with the prophecies, poetry and ethics of the Bible is as essential to the educated man of today as was a "knowledge of Greek history in the time of Pericles or of English History in the reign of Henry VIII." In keeping with this view, there has been put into the book only a minimum of matter calculated to take the student away from the Bible itself to a discussion about it, and a maximum of such matter as will require him to study the Scripture first hand.

The general plan is the outgrowth of several years of experience in teaching which indicates that the type of students for which it is intended are interested in the facts and in the conclusions reached, but care little as to how the conclusions were reached. The material has, therefore, been carefully gathered from any and all reliable sources and lays little claim to originality. But due acknowledgement is here made for all suggestions and help coming from all sources whatsoever.

Let it be further said that in preparing these studies the author has proceeded on the basis of a belief in the Bible as the Word of God, a true source of comfort for every condition of heart and a safe guide to all faith and conduct whether of individuals or of nations. It is hoped, therefore, that those who may study the topics presented will approach the Scripture with an open heart, that it may have full power to make them feel the need of God, that they may make its provisions real in their experience and that it may bring to them new and changed lives.

If the pastors shall deem it valuable as a book of references for themselves and for their members who are desirous of pursuing Bible study, or if it shall be found serviceable to any or all of those mentioned in the paragraph describing those for whom it was intended, the author will be amply rewarded for the effort made.

J. B. TIDWELL.

Waco, Texas.

SUGGESTIONS TO TEACHERS, LEADERS, AND CLASSES

CONCERNING CLASSES IN THE SCHOOLS

1. **For Academy Classes.** The work has been laid out with a view to making one unit of college entrance credit. Follow the lessons as outlined, which will require: (1) a mastery of all the introductory discussions; (2) the mastery of the main points (indicated by I, II, etc.) of the analysis of the books; (3) the memory of the messages based on each book; (4) the reading of the Scripture assignments and the study of the topics: "For Study and Discussion."

2. **For College Classes.** College classes should do all that is suggested for Academy Classes and in addition: (1) the whole analysis of each book should be mastered and in some cases worked out in greater detail; (2) other topics for study and investigation should be assigned with written reports and themes; (3) library work should be assigned touching the discussions and topics on each book; (4) make much of Scripture proof texts.

CONCERNING OTHER STUDENTS OR CLASSES

For other classes such as Sunday school classes or women's and young people's societies and for individuals the work may be begun anywhere. Choice should be made of some one book or group of books and the work divided into fewer or more lessons as the time to be given and the purpose of the study may require. After the introductory notes have been read and mastered the student may: (1) follow the analysis as topics with free discussions; (2) study the Scripture to verify the messages of the book; (3) search out the information sought in the topics "For Study and Discussion."

GENERAL SUGGESTIONS

(1) Vary the procedure. One time let the student read the Scripture to verify the messages. Another time let the teacher make them the basis of lectures. (2) Have some of the work on the topics done in writing and submitted for correction. (3) Drill the class in concert on the facts, analysis and messages. (4) Review often (5) Have occasional written tests.

CONTENTS

Introductory Matters

INTRODUCTORY MATTERS

In this chapter the student is introduced to four subjects, the study of which should greatly aid both in the ease and in the intelligence with which he studies the Bible itself.

THE NAMES OF GOD

In the Old Testament several names are used for God. Each of these has a special significance derived from the Hebrew meaning of the word. And while the student can not always distinguish the exact meaning, he should in a general way know the meaning of each name. The following, while not all the names and though not fully expressing the meaning, will be of use to us:

1. God. This word comes from one word and two of its compounds or forms and will mean accordingly: (1) The Strong One, indicating that God is a great, strong, or powerful being. This term is used 225 times in the Old Testament. (2) The Strong One as an object of worship. If God is all-powerful and we are without strength, it behooves us to worship Him. (3) The Strong One who is faithful and therefore to be trusted and obeyed. He is not only strong but keeps all His covenants and is, therefore, worthy of our confidence. This last term is plural and is used 2,300 times in the Old Testament. It is the name used when God said "Let us make man" and "God created man in his own image," etc. (Gen. 1:26-27). By this name God, the Trinity, covenanted for the good of man before he was created.

2. LORD. In the old version all the letters are small capitals. In the revised version it is translated Jehovah. It means: (1) God, the Self-existing One who reveals Himself. He always existed, and yet condescended to reveal

Himself to man. (2) God as Redeemer. The purpose of the revelation of Himself is to bring us redemption. It was under this name that He sought man after the fall and clothed him with the skin of animals, Gen. 3:9-17. (3) God who makes and keeps His covenants. This name was used more than one hundred times in connection with the covenants, as in Jer. 31:31-34, where He promises a new covenant.

3. **Lord.** Here all the letters are small except L, and the word is the same in old and new versions. It refers to God in His relation to men as His servants. There are two kinds of servants referred to in the passages—the hired servant and the bought servant. The latter is always superior and far more beloved than the former. The relations here implied are very suggestive. The master has a right to expect respect and obedience from the servant, and the servant is guaranteed direction and protection and support from the master. As applied to us and God it indicates our duty to serve Him and assures us that He will provide for and protect us.

4. **Almighty God.** The translation here does not at all convey the meaning intended. It does not refer primarily to strength. That is found in the term God. But this word suggests a figure common among the ancients. It means literally a Strong-Breasted One. It refers to God as the Pourer forth or Shedder forth of blessings, both spiritual and temporal. It suggests that God is: (1) Nourisher, Strength Giver, Satisfier. He is the Strong One who gives. Just as a mother nourishes her babe at her bosom and pours into it the strength of her own life, just as in that way she gives to it strength and satisfaction; so God feeds and satisfies us out of the fullness of His own nature. (2) Giver of fruitfulness. This is the proper and normal result of the nourishment. God supplies us with spiritual food and we should thereby give returns. He was to make Abraham fruitful, Gen. 17:1-8. This was absolutely unconditional and was completely fulfilled. (3) Giver of chas-

tening or pruning. This was another step in the same direction. If fruit is desired the tree must be pruned as well as nourished. God sometimes chastens us that we may be more useful to Him.

5. **The Most High God.** The meaning of this term may be summed up in two points: (1) It represents God as the Possessor of heaven and earth. Because He possesses the earth He acts within His rights and distributes it among the several nations, Deut. 32:8. (2) It represents God as having all authority. If He possesses it all, He has the right of dominion over both the earth and the man to whom it has been distributed, Dan. 4:18, 37; Ps. 91:9-13.

6. **Everlasting God.** This represents Him: (1) As the God of the mystery of the ages. (2) As the God of all secrets. (3) As the God of everlasting existence, whose understanding is past finding out, Isa. 40:28. Here is a great joy for the believer. There are so many secrets and mysteries, but our God understands and sees them all. Nothing is beyond His knowledge. Here is our joy in trusting and following Him through the unknown.

7. **LORD (Jehovah) God.** This name of Deity is used of two relations: (1) Of the relation of Deity to man. In this use there are suggested three things concerning this relation: (a) That He is Creator and creates and controls man's destiny, especially emphasizing His control of the earthly relations; (b) That He has moral authority over man; (c) That He is man's Redeemer. These three ideas indicate something of the divine interest in us. (2) Of the relation of Deity to Israel. In this it is implied that He made and controlled her destiny.

8. **LORD (Jehovah) of Hosts.** This name speaks of Jehovah as Lord of warrior hosts or in His manifestation of power. It has three special suggestions. (1) It usually refers to the hosts of heaven, especially of angels. (2) It refers to all the divine and heavenly power available for the people of God. (3) It is the special name of Deity used

to comfort Israel in time of division and defeat or failure, Isa. 1:9; 8:11-14. This name is never used in the Pentateuch, and is used especially by the prophets. It is used 80 times by Jeremiah, 14 times in the two chapters of Haggai, 50 times in the fourteen chapters of Zechariah, 25 times in the four chapters of Malachi.

There are a number of other compound names used to express the different relations and blessings of Jehovah and His works for men. But they are of less frequent use and their meaning is often easily understood. Those given above seem to be sufficient to aid the student in reading.

THE SACRED OFFICERS

There are a number of sacred officers to whom the Bible makes frequent reference. At least the following outstanding facts about each of them should be familiar to all Bible students:

1. **The Priests.** These were men chosen to appear before God for the people whose sins disqualified them from appearing in their own behalf. The first priests were the heads of their households, Gen. 8:20. Later, the first born or eldest son became the priest. And finally, in order that the priesthood might be properly recognized, God chose the family of Aaron of the tribe of Levi for priests of His own chosen nation, Ex. 28:1. They served in the tabernacle and later in the temple, where they conducted religious services, offered sacrifices for public and private sins, and were teachers and magistrates of the law.

2. **The Prophets.** (1) These were men whose work may be thought of as the complement of that done by the priests. They spoke to the people for God. While priests plead the cause of the people before God, prophets plead the cause of God before the people. They received revelations from God and made them known to the people. They were selected according to God's own will to impart

His spiritual gifts (1 Cor. 12:11) and extended their activities down through the years and included those who wrote the prophetic books to Malachi. (2) They were philosophers, teachers, preachers, and guides of the people's piety and worship. Their work may be divided into three kinds: (a) The utterance of public discourse very much as the preacher of today; (b) The writing of the history and biography and annals of their nation, whereby we have the Old Testament; (c) The discernment of the future. In this capacity they were called seers and foretold events that should afterwards transpire. Abraham was the first to be called a prophet (Gen. 20:7) and Aaron next (Ex. 7:1).

3. **The Scribes.** The word scribe means writer, and Seraiah is the first one mentioned, II Sam. 8:17. (1) As writers they soon became transcribers of the law, then interpreters, and finally the teachers and expounders of it. (2) They became known as lawyers. This grew out of their knowledge of the law which was acquired by their frequent copying of it. (3) This led the people to accord to them a place of high standing and dignity, and in the time of the kings they were supported by the state as a learned, well-organized and highly influential body of men. (4) In the time of Christ they were among the most influential members of the Sanhedrin.

4. **The Apostles.** (1) These were twelve men chosen by Jesus and formed the foundation or beginning of Christ's Church. They were separate from all the Old Testament orders and were, therefore, under no obligation to caste. Nor were they bound to the old administration of things. (2) The name apostle means a messenger, or one sent. They were chosen to be with Jesus and to be sent forth by Him to preach and teach. (3) When Judas, one of the twelve, betrayed Him and "departed unto his own place," they elected Matthias to take his place (Acts 1:15-26). Paul was later appointed in a special way (Acts 9:1-30). Barnabas was called an apostle (Acts 14:14), and others also seemed to have been so designated. (4) These men

led new movements (Acts 5:12-13) and devoted themselves especially to ministerial gifts (Acts 8:14-18). They had first authority in the Church (Acts 9:27; 15-2; I Cor. 9:1; 12:28; II Cor. 10:8; 12:2; Gal. 1:17; 2:8-9).

5. **Ministers or Preachers.** (1) The word minister here means one who ministers to or aids another in service. This they do as free attendants and not as slaves. (2) They became teachers, and hence our term minister (Acts 13:2; Rom. 15:16). (3) Today they are preachers and teachers of the Word of God and minister to the spiritual needs of God's people and of others.

THE SACRED OCCASIONS

The occasions which are hallowed in the Scriptures are of much interest. They set forth certain great conceptions and purposes that are worthy of special consideration. Indeed, it is necessary to know their import, if we are to grasp quickly the meaning of certain passages. The following are the important ones:

1. **The Sabbath.** It is difficult to define the term. But it means something like "a solemn rest" (Lev. 25:4). The first mention of it is found in Gen. 2:2-3, and the first mention of the weekly Sabbath is found in Ex. 16:22-30. It is again suggested in the division of weeks (Gen. 8:10-12; 29:27-28), and Israel was finally commanded to keep it (Ex. 20:8-11). It is clearly used to indicate our need of a day in which to rest from life's toil and to worship.

2. **The New Moons.** These were special feasts held on the first day of the month (Num. 10:10), and were celebrated with the offering of sacrifices (Num. 28:11-15). Among the northern tribes the time of the New Moon feast was regarded as propitious for going to the prophet for instruction, II Kings 4:23.

3. The Annual Feasts. The Jews had several annual feasts, as follows: (1) The Passover Feast. This was celebrated on April 14 (Ex. 12:1-51) and commemorated the deliverance out of Egypt and the saving of the first born of the Jews. (2) The Feast of Pentecost. This came on June 6 (Ex. 34:22; Lev. 23:15-16; Deut. 16:9-10; Num. 28: 26-31, and commemorated the giving of the law. (3) The Feast of Trumpets. This was on October 1 (Lev. 23:23-25; Num. 29:1-6) and marked the beginning of the civil year. (4) The Day of Atonement. This occurred on October 10 (Lev. 16:1-34; 23:27-32). The purpose was to make atonement for the sins of the people. (5) The Feast of Tabernacles. This lasted a week (Lev. 23:34-43; Ex. 23:16; 34:22; Deut. 16:13-15) and was kept in memory of Israel's life and experiences in the wilderness wanderings. All the outstanding matters of these years were emblemized. (6) The Feast of Dedication, which was celebrated December 25 (I Kings 8:2; II Chron. 5:3). This was kept in commemoration of the dedication of the temple. It seems to have originated following the rebuilding of the temple, but probably came to include the thought of the dedication of Solomon's temple also. (7) The Feast of Purim. This memorialized the deliverance of the Jews through Easter (Est. 9: 20-32) and was observed on March 14 and 15.

4. The Sabbatical Year. This came every seventh year, and all the land of Israel was to rest just as the people of Israel rested every seventh day. No seed was to be sown and all that grew was public property and could be taken by the poor at will. During that year all debts were to be forgiven except those against foreigners (Ex. 23:10-11; Lev. 25:2-7; Deut. 15:1-11).

5. The Year of Jubilee. Every fiftieth years was known as the Year of Jubilee (Lev. 25:8-55). It began on the tenth day of the seventh month, and during it the soil remained untilled just as during the Sabbatical year. All the land that had been sold and alienated went back to the original owner, and all the Hebrew slaves became free, if they desired such freedom.

6. The Lord's Day. It is the first day of the week and is observed in commemoration of the resurrection of Jesus, which occurred on that day. It also celebrated the finished work of redemption, just as the Sabbath was kept in commemoration of the finishing of the work of creation.

THE SACRED INSTITUTIONS OF WORSHIP

The following institutions of worship are often referred to in the Bible, and to know something of the history and significance of each will be found helpful.

1. The Altar. There are here several matters for study. (1) The first direct mention of it, Gen. 8:20. (2) The different persons who are mentioned as erecting altars, Gen. 1—Ex. 20. (3) Materials used in constructing the altar, Ex. 20:24-25. (4) The purpose for which altars were erected, including that of Joshua, Josh. 22:10, 22-29.

2. The Tabernacle. The description is given in Exodus, chapters 25 to 29. Our study of it should include: (1) The instructions to build it, including the offerings and articles to be given. (2) Its erection and the furnishings which it was to have in it. (3) Its purpose, Ex. 29:42-45; Heb. chaps. 9-10. (4) Its history—where it was first set up, how long used, etc.

3. The Temple. Around the temple clusters much of the hope and aspiration of the nation. There were three temples in all. (1) Solomon's temple. In connection with this temple there are several fields of study: (a) David's desire to build it and his preparation for it, II Sam. 7:1-2; I Chron., chaps. 28-29. (b) Its material, erection, and dedication, I Kings 5:8; II Chron. 2:6. (c) Its destruction by the general of Nebuchadnezzar, 587 B. C. (2) Zerubbabel's temple. Here we should study the decree of Cyrus; the return of the Jews, the rebuilding and dedication of the temple, Ezra, chaps. 1-6; its destruction by Pompey, 63 B. C., and by Herod the Great, 37 B. C. (3) Herod's temple. This temple was begun 20 or 21 B. C., John 2:20, and destroyed by Titus A. D. 70.

4. **The Synagogue.** The Greek word from which it is derived means "an assemblage." It was originated rather late in the history of the nation, but soon came to have a most important place in its religious life. Synagogues were built wherever faithful Jews went. In the time of Christ, or not long before, there were about 1,500 in Palestine, with perhaps 480 in Jerusalem. It seems to have had three officers: (1) The Ruler, Luke 8:49; 13:14; Mark 5:22, etc. (2) The Elders, Luke 7:3; Matt. 15:2, etc. (3) The Minister, Luke 4:20. The service was very simple and consisted of prayer and of reading and expounding the Scriptures. These synagogues and their worship were of great advantage to the Apostles in their work, furnishing them with an opportunity to teach Christianity wherever they went.

5. **The Church.** This is a New Testament term. Up to Christ's time no such thing as a church existed. The word means "an assemblage," and is most commonly used to designate a local congregation of Christian workers. It is sometimes spoken of as the "Church of Christ," the "Church of God," the "Saints," etc. Churches were established in various cities and often had their meeting places in some private home. It is not proper to call all the Christians of a particular denomination a church. And again, it would be wrong to call all the Christians of any denomination in a given territory a church. As, for instance, it would be wrong to speak of the Baptist Church of the South. The Bible usually speaks of it as the church at Corinth, and if it speaks of it otherwise at all, it refers to a larger conception. By a study of the principal churches and leaders of Christian movements after the ascension of Jesus, we can get a rather clear understanding of the New Testament idea of the church.

SEVEN GREAT COVENANTS

There are two kinds of covenants. (1) Declarative or unconditional, example, Gen. 9:11, "I will." (2) Mutual or conditional, example, Ex. 19:5, "If thou wilt." All Scripture is a development of or is summed up in the seven covenants.

1. **The Adamic Covenant,** Gen. 3:14-19. Outline the elements of the covenant, showing the persons affected and the results or conditions involved.

2. **The Noahic Covenant,** Gen. 8:20—9:27. Outline the elements of the covenant, and the results involved.

3. **The Abrahamic Covenant,** Gen. 12:1-3; Acts 7:3; other details, Gen. 13:14-17; 15:1-18; 17:1-8. Outline, giving the elements, blessings proposed, temporal and spiritual or eternal. This is sometimes called several covenants, but it seems best to consider it one that is enlarged upon from time to time.

4. **The Mosaic Covenant,** Ex. 19—30. Given in two parts: (1) **Law of Duty** (Ten Commandments), (2) **Law of Mercy,** Priesthood and Sacrifices, Lev. 4:27-31; Heb. 9:1-7. (3) To whom given, Ex. 19:3 and to all, Rom. 2:12; 3:19, etc. (4) Its purpose: (a) Negative, Rom. 3:19-20; Gal. 2:16-21, etc. (b) Positive, Rom. 3:19; 7:7-13. (5) Christ's relation to the Mosaic covenant: (a) Was under it, Gal. 4:4; Matt. 3:13, etc.; (b) Kept it, John 8:46; 15:10; (c) Bore its curse for sinners, Gal. 3:10-13; 4:4-5; II Cor. 5:21, etc.; (d) Took the place of and ended the Priesthood and Sacrifices, Heb. 9:11-15; 10:1-12, etc.; (e) New covenant provided for believers in Christ, Rom. 8:1; Gal. 3:13-17.

5. **The Deuteronomic Covenant,** Deut. 30:1-9. Outline its elements, giving things promised and prophesied.

6. The Davidic Covenant, II Sam. 7:5-19. (1) Elements of the covenant and summary in the Old Testament. (2) In the New Testament.

7. The New Covenant. (1) Formed, Heb. 8:6-13. (2) In prophecy, Jer. 31:31-34. (3) It is founded on the sacrifice of Christ, Matt. 26:27-28; I Cor. 11:25; Heb. 9:11-12. (4) It is primarily for Israel, but Christians are partakers, Heb. 10:11-22; Eph. 2:11-20. (5) Jews are yet to be brought into it, Ezek. 20:34-37; Jer. 23:5-6; Rom. 11:25-27.

Note. Try to see how all of these covenants met in Christ.

INSPIRATION OF THE BIBLE

1. **Scripture Claims.** II Tim. 3:16 says: "All Scripture is given by inspiration of God." The word inspired comes from two Greek words and literally means God-breathed. The term "given by inspiration" teaches that the Scriptures are the result of some kind of influence which God exerted on the writers. Moreover, it means a conscious breathing. According to this passage, then, inspiration means a strong and conscious inbreathing of God into men by which they are qualified to give utterance to truth. It is God speaking through men making the Scriptures as much the word of God as if He had spoken it through His own lips. By the infusion of the breath of God, holy men of God wrote in obedience to the divine command and were kept from all error. This was true whether they were writing some new truth or recording truth formerly known. The Bible, then, is the very word of God, and its several books are of divine origin and authority.

2. **Some Theories of Inspiration.** In the study of this question one meets many theories. (1) Some count it a sort of "genius of high order." They deny that there is anything supernatural connected with the action of the Spirit upon Scripture writers, and assert or imply that their inspiration is to be compared with that of Milton or Shakespeare or Brownng or Confucius, that God dwells in all men and all men are therefore inspired, each to a degree measured by his mental or spiritual capacity. This should be absolutely rejected. (2) Some think that their inspiration was like that of the Christian age. Such a theory would make any ordinary Christian of today as much inspired as was Peter or John or Paul. This would be mere illumination instead of infallible guidance into truth, and leaves

room for varying degrees of truth and error. Such a theory would count it possible for some of us to produce a new Bible today—an idea which our own sense of insufficiency denies. (3) Some claim that it was altogether mechanical. This has the idea that the writers were robbed of their own individuality and became nothing but passive instruments or machines. But this theory fails to account for the differences of style and the peculiarities of the writers such as the use of cultured or uncultured style and the use of terminology of the country or city, which are everywhere manifest, and make it impossible for us to harmonize the theory with the Scriptures. There are several other theories, each of which is fully as unsatisfactory as these.

3. **The Real Meaning.** It should be said that no theory can be regarded as exhaustive. We cannot completely analyze all of the processes of the Holy Spirit operating on the minds of men. But if we study the many Scriptures that bear upon the subject, we shall find that some of them claim to be the very words and writings of God Himself, spoken by His own mouth or written with His own hand; some seem to have been spoken by men who were unconscious of the full meaning of their message; some were written after diligent and faithful investigation on the part of the writer. The Holy Spirit used "the attention, the investigation, the memory, the fancy, the logic—in a word, all the faculties of the writer, and wrought through these. He guided the writer to choose what narrative and materials, speeches of others, imperial decrees, genealogies, official letters, state papers, or historical matter he found necessary for the recording of the divine message of salvation. He wrought in and with and through their spirits. He used the men themselves, and spoke through their individualities. This He also did in the prediction of future events.

It should also be said that inspiration affected the very words. For it would be hardly possible for inspiration to insure the correct transmission of thought without in some way affecting the words. God so controlled the writers in the expression of His thought that they gave us the word of God in the language of men. And, being directed by an infallible guide, they kept out all error in the statement of facts. It is then as truly God's own word as if He had used no instrument at all in writing it. The ideas it expresses are the very ideas which God wanted to convey, so that God is fully responsible for every word of it. Paul teaches this by saying he spoke in the word which the Holy Ghost teacheth (I Cor. 2:13).

SCRIPTURE CANON

1. **Meaning of the Term Canon.** The word translated canon comes from a Greek word meaning "a straight rod" or "a measuring rule." From this it derives the secondary meaning, "line." "rule," and even "law." Later, it came to mean a list, or catalogue. It soon came to be used as the standard of opinion or of action, and was finally applied to the books of the Bible. Then there came into use terms "Old Testament Canon" and "New Testament Canon." Two ideas are involved. (1) It is the canon of truth. In this sense it refers to the restriction of the number of books that compose the Bible. It is a collection of those books which are inspired of God and through and in which He speaks and by the Spirit appeals to the human heart and conscience. (2) It is the rule of faith and life. Since it is "a measuring rod," it leads us to think of the Scriptures as a rule for our lives. It is used in this sense in Gal. 6:16 and Phl. 3:16.

2. **Why a Canon Was Formed.** There were three causes that operated to make it necessary to form the Canon of the Bible. (1) To preserve the inspired writings from corruption. There was no pressing need for the canon while the voice of the prophet and apostle was still to be heard. They by inspiration knew what was truly inspired and what was not. But as soon they died and inspiration ceased, it was necessary to gather up their books

and thereby preserve their message to the people, and assure them against corruption. (2) To prevent the addition of other books. There had already appeared many other writings claimed to be inspired. The question had arisen as to what was the extent of inspiration, and it became necessary to decide which books were really inspired. (3) To prevent any attempt to destroy the Bible. When Emperor Diocletian in A. D. 302 issued an edict to have all these sacred books burned, the question arose as to which of them were inspired and sacred.

3. **Canon of the Old Testament.** The Old Testament was formed among the Jews and was later taken over by the Christians. While it is not possible to determine with certainty the exact steps by which it grew into its final form, we are certain that it was a gradual formation, composed of books which spread over many centuries. The Law was collected and placed in the Ark of the Covenant by the command of Moses. Next, it seems that the historical and prophetical books from Joshua to David's time were placed in the temple. From time to time the sacred list was increased. The most ancient Jewish writings declare that the canon as we now have it was the work of Ezra and the great Synagogue composed of Ezra, Nehemiah, Haggai, Zechariah, and Malachi. There is no doubt that such a collection existed in the time of Jesus and the Apostles. Its formation was not an arbitrary act, but it was submitted by the people to an official council for action, the final action being about A. D. 90, by the council of Jamnia.

4. **Canon of the New Testament.** It was in the sixteenth century before there was any such general action with reference to the New Testament books which could be accepted with binding authority. The principle underlying the formation of the New Testament Canon is, as in the Old Testament, the fact of inspiration. (1) The death of the Apostles made necessary the collection so that their writings might be preserved and their authority recognized. There had

arisen the epistolary literature as well as the gospels, and their message could only be kept inviolate by the formation of the canon. (2) At the time of the severe persecution (302 A. D.), there had arisen many writers and many false and spurious gospels and epistles which were asking for acceptance as genuine. The persecutors demanded that the Scriptures be given up. But the Christians refused to comply with the demand. This, however, raised the question as to which books were the inspired writings of Apostles and others. (3) There were many local councils, such as the Council of Laodicea, about 360 A. D., and the Third Council of Carthage, 397 A. D. Thus, by continued councils and by careful, prayerful and deliberate examination, they finally proved which were true and which were false, and as a result we have the New Testament.

VERSIONS OF THE BIBLE

1. Languages of the Bible. With the exception of a very few passages, the Old Testament was written in Hebrew, which was especially the language of the children of Israel. The New Testament was written in Greek. Soon after the Bible was completed, these languages ceased to be of common use and were counted among the dead languages. Thus was the word of God left in a permanent form so that all people in all times and places may come and find a divine revelation in the same fixed and unchangeable form. Moreover, these two languages are the very highest and most perfect development of the two great families of speech (the Semitic and the Indo-Germanic), and are the richest of all languages in their spiritual import.

2. Value of a Knowledge of the Original Languages. One can hardly fail to see that there would be great value in knowing the original languages. No translation can take the place of the original. It could not be a full translation unless one could apprehend and convey the very spirit of the original text. One must think and feel as the original authors; one's mind must move in the same channels of thought; one must adapt oneself to the various types of character of the divine revelation before one can apprehend the thought of revelation and make it one's own. These considerations should impress us with something of the importance of a knowledge of the two Bible languages. If the churches are to maintain a living connection with the deeper things of Scripture, they must not allow the study of these languages to fall into disuse. Especially should we insist that our ministers shall have more than a superficial knowledge of the divine Word. They should have a thorough acquaintance with the original sources and perennial fountains of truth. If we fail at this point, the life of our people will be cut off from the original sources of spiritual growth and the interpretations of one generation or group will assume the place and importance of the divine Word, and mechanical institutions of human contrivance will take the place of "living communion with God."

It should be said, however, that, important as this is, one may, although deprived of it, drink deep at the fountain of truth. Only a comparatively small number can know at first hand the niceties of meaning suggested by the words and phrases used in the Holy Writings. Yet through the labors of others, we and the men of almost all the nations and tribes can now read the Bible in our own language. We may thus learn of the wonderful work of grace which God has manifested. We may miss much of the beauty and suggestiveness, and yet the English reader, with nothing but the English Bible, may, by trusting the guidance of the Holy Spirit, understand it far better than the critical scholar who leaves out the Spirit and trusts only to his natural sagacity. We may therefore rejoice that we have translations from the original.

3. **Ancient Versions.** There were translations of the Old Testament before the beginning of the Christian era. This was necessary, first, because the Jews, being scattered among other people, began to adopt their language;

and second, because even in Palestine the Aramaic language began to displace the Hebrew. As the Christians multiplied it soon became necessary to translate the New Testament also. There are two groups here: (1) The Old Testament versions. Four may be mentioned: (a) The Septuagint, a translation of the Old Testament into Greek, begun about 250 B. C. (b) Version of Aquila, in opposition to the Septuagint, which had been appropriated by Christians. It was made some time in the second century A. D. (c) The Version of Theodotian, which was made during the second century A. D., and corrected many inaccuracies in the Septuagint. (d) The Version of Symmachus, who with much elegance of style and language, paraphrased the Septuagint about 200 A. D. (2) The Old and New Testament Versions: (a) The Peshito. This is the best of the Syriac versions of the Scriptures and was made for the use of Syrian Christians. It seems to have been produced in the second century A. D., and was largely in use by the latter part of the fourth century. (b) The Vulgate. This was a Latin version, made by Jerome (383-405 A. D.). It was made to take the place of the earlier Latin translations made from the Septuagint. Both the Peshito and the Vulgate contain the Old and New Testaments.

4. **English Versions.** (1) The early translations. During the period from the sixth to the thirteenth century, there were many partial and imperfect translations. Indeed, one complete translation is mentioned, but nothing is known of it. It was the thirteenth century before we find worthy and lasting translations. Here we have one great work—the translation of Wycliffe. It was a translation from the Latin Vulgate (1380 A. D.), and contained the whole Bible. It was a protest against the evil of his age. He was tried for this work while he was alive, and after his death his body was exhumed and burned by his enemies. (2) Translations during the period of the Reformation. The Reformation gave a new impetus toward giving the Bible to the whole people. The translation of the

Bible into the vernacular of the people would show them how very unscriptural were a large portion of the practices and teachings of the priests and friars. Much of the time of the Reformers was therefore given to translation. The most important of these translations are as follows: (a) Tyndale's New Testament (1525 A. D.), followed later by portions of the Old Testament. This was the first attempt to translate the whole Bible from the Greek and Hebrew. It created such bitter opposition from the Papal power that he was burned at the stake in 1536. (b) Miles Coverdale. This was the first complete English translation ever printed. It was partly original and partly a revision of Tyndale's work and appeared in 1535. It does not profess to have been made from the original languages. (c) Other versions. Following these there appeared many translations. Matthew's Bible, which was edited by John Rogers, appeared in 1537. Other editions of that period were those by Travener, in 1539, and The Great Bible (so called because of the size of its pages), edited by Thomas Cromwell in 1539, and Bishop's Bible, which was a revison of the Great Bible, appeared in 1568. Another and different version of this time is the Geneva Bible, which was published by some refugees whom Queen Mary had driven out of her country. It gained a wide circulation among the people, one or more editions appearing each year from 1560 to 1616. (3) The King James or Authorized Version. This version is the result of the labor of fifty-four divines chosen by King James. The commission of these men was issued in 1607 and the great work was completed in 1611. Its sterling value and beautiful language soon gave it a supremacy which it has always held. It is impossible to estimate the value of this great version. (4) The Revised Version. Because several new manuscripts had been discovered and because there had been changes in the meaning of English words and because scholarship had advanced and was better able to get the meaning of the ancient languages, it was thought wise to undertake a new translation. The most distinguished scholars of all Protestant denominations of both England and the United States were secured for the work. The English revisers divided themselves into two groups, one for the Old Testament and the other for the New. There were two like groups in America also. The broad outline of the work was laid down in 1870. The results of the work of the English groups were submitted to the American groups, who could make suggestions, but the final decisions rested with the English groups. However, the suggestions that were not adopted were published in an appendix. The revised New Testament appeared in 1881 and the entire Bible in 1885. (5) The American Revised Version. This is by most modern scholars thought to be the best version yet produced. The English committee rejected many of the suggestions of the American groups. But they were, as stated above, printed in an appendix. In compensation for this favor, the American scholars pledged themselves that for fourteen years they would not sanction the publication of any editions of the revised versions not printed by the University Press of England. After the publication in 1885 the English committees soon dissolved, but the American committees resolved to continue their organization and work. There was a feeling that the value of their suggestions would yet be seen and that they would be given a place in the text. It was soon seen that there would come a demand for such a course. In 1898, one year before the period of their agreement had ended, there was issued in England the so-called American Revised Version, which transferred the American preferences from the appendix to the text itself. But the American revisers had been busy all these years in an attempt to improve the entire revised version, and the English "American Revised Version" did not satisfy them. They therefore published in 1901 the "Standard Edition of the American Revised Version," which is far more accurate than the revised version of 1885.

5. **Future Versions.** We may expect that other versions will appear in the future as the need shall arise for them.

And the need will certainly arise. Our language changes and words come to have new and different meanings and would not convey to the reader the proper meaning unless from time to time it should be revised and expressed according to those new meanings. This changefulness of language that is being used suggests the divine wisdom of depositing the word of God in dead languages. It remains always the same and will always mean the same to all people. But it will have to be expressed differently and will require new translations. Being in the dead languages, it is the eternal, unchangeable word of God, and being translated into other and modern languages it lives for all people according to the terms of the living language which they use. Let us then not be afraid of new versions except to be certain that they are true to the meaning of the original language in which the divine truth was left.

THE DIVISION OF THE BIBLE

In language and contents, the Bible is divided into two main divisions:

(1) The Old Testament, 39 Books. (2) The New Testament, 27 Books. Total, 66 Books.

The Jews were accustomed to divide the Old Testament into three main parts, as follows:

1. **The Law** — The first five books, Genesis to Deuteronomy, otherwise called the Pentateuch and books of Moses.

2. **The Prophets.** These are divided into the "former prophets" or historical books, and the "later prophets," or books which we commonly call the prophetic books.

3. **The Writings,** which was made to include: (1) Poetical books — Psalms, Proverbs, and Job; (2) Five Rolls — Song of Solomon, Ruth, Esther, Lamentations, and Ecclesiastes; (3) Other Books—Daniel, Ezra, Nehemiah, and I and II Chronicles.

The Bible itself divides the Old Testament into the three following divisions:

1. **The Law,** which includes the first five books of the Bible, also called the books of Moses.

2. **The Prophets,** which includes the next twelve books, commonly called historical books, and the seventeen books we know as the prophetic books.

3. **The Psalms,** including the five poetical books.

THE BOOKS OF THE BIBLE

The books of the Old and New Testaments may each be divided into three or five groups as follows:

First into three groups:

1. **History.**
   (1) Old Testament—Genesis-Esther (17 books).
   (2) New Testament—Matthew-Acts (5 books).
2. **Doctrine**
   (1) Old Testament—Job-Song of Solomon (5 books).
   (2) New Testament—Romans-Jude (21 books).
3. **Prophecy**
   (1) Old Testament—Isaiah-Malachi (17 books).
   (2) New Testament—Revelation (1 book).

Second, into five groups:

1. **Old Testament.**
   (1) Pentateuch—Genesis-Deuteronomy (5 books).
   (2) Historical Books—Joshua-Esther (12 books).
   (3) Poetical Books—Job-Song of Solomon (5 books).
   (4) Major Prophets—Isaiah-Daniel (5 books).
   (5) Minor Prophets—Hosea-Malachi (12 books).
2. **New Testament.**
   (1) Gospels—Matthew-John (4 books).
   (2) Acts—Acts (1 book).
   (3) Pauline Epistles—Romans-Herbews (14 books).
   (4) General Epistles—James Jude (7 books).
   (5) **Revelation—Revelation (1 book).**

A WONDERFUL BOOK

Without a doubt, the Bible is the most wonderful book in all the world. We see it so commonly that we are apt to forget the world of blessing it has brought to our race. For about two thousand five hundred years of human history there was no Bible. There was no written revelation from God, and only occasional direct and personal revelations of His will to men. But finally He gave this book to guide us in ways that are acceptable to Him. It is a book of great interest, revealing matters of the deepest concern to all men. It is a book of life and preserves something of the spirit of Him who produced it. In reading it we feel the great Spirit of the Author touch our spirit and change our life to one like His. We marvel at its power.

1. Its Wonderful History. It is a history of surpassing wonder. It differs from all other history in that its history is subordinate in purpose, being used only as it is necessary in revealing God and His will to mankind. Whether the matter recorded is personal, or tribal, or national, a high religious purpose stands forth pre-eminent, and one is impressed that the very heart of the history is a revelation of saving grace and reveals the loving heart of God.

It is then a history that shows the proper relation of cause and effect, and that from the standpoint of divine religion. It is intended to promote a true understanding of a living union between God and man, and to help men live a life that will reflect the nature and works of God as well as something of His purity and holiness. It furnishes a history of the unfolding in the mind of man and under the influence and presence of the Divine One all those fine moral and religious principles that have come to be the source of our highest and best progress. It is the history of the revelation and working out of a divine plan of human redemption. It is a history of principles and conduct for the governing of men, conceived by God as good for them, as those principles are worked out in human experience.

To study this wonderful history is our inspiring task. We are to learn not only the story, but the sacred meaning and messages of the rise and fall of nations. We are to behold the overthrow of the wicked and the preservation, through His grace, of the chosen people. It is to be a continuous illustration of the reality and blessing of divine providence as we see in the conflict of nations the gradual preparation of the world for the final coming of Jesus, the Universal Man, the Son of God, and our Saviour. Such a study should impress the student with the sacredness of all human life and should create in him a reverence for the God of our destinies.

2. **Its Beautiful Morals.** Here is a moral system that is absolutely worthy, both in form and substance. It has the Bible for its basis and the life of Jesus for its illustration. It is a system of morals based upon the deepest religious sanctions, a system absolutely right, because the religion upon which it rests is perfect. It roots its moral principles in the personality of God, who is perfect and supreme, and who alone is the source of moral obligation. He can, and does, therefore, give us moral precepts of the highest beauty.

These perfect moral principles contain both negative and positive teachings. (1) Negative teachings. Indeed, no other book but the Bible can so boldly proclaim to us "thou shalt not." But it directs us in ways that will prevent us from injuring ourselves or other people. It would keep us from false worship, from sinful desires, and from self-ambition, all of which are calculated to do us special spiritual harm. On the other hand, it would keep us back from covetousness, anger, revenge, contemptuous speech, censoriousness, swearing, lying, stealing, murder, and blasphemy, all of which would especially harm us. (2) Positive commands. The Bible gives due emphasis to every moral obligation resting upon us. It begins with our duty to God, which cannot be accomplished except by love to Him. It then teaches us to love our neighbor as ourselves, and shows how these two things are so closely related that the latter cannot exist except as the result of the former. To put it a little more fully, it enjoins duties having to do especially with God, such as repentance and faith and worship; duties related particularly to self, such as humility, patience, courage, and self-sacrifice; duties having to do with the family, such as faithfulness on the part of husband and wife, and filial and parental love; duties that are general, such as forgiveness, kindness to enemies, help for the needy, patriotism, and business integrity. To learn of these beautiful ethics is a part of our task.

3. **Its Glorious Christ and Eternal Life.** In all the Bible we are led to consider Jesus, who, in speaking of the Old Testament, said it spake of Him. No other study is so glorious because no other person is so glorious. To fail to prize Him is to be blind to the best of all lives and to the divine and only Saviour. Here also we are to learn of the eternal life which He provides for all men, and are to find our duty to bring knowledge of it to others. Our study should lead the unsaved to become Christians, and should lead Christians to become winners of others. The Bible will reveal ample rewards for the service.

In the light of all this, what a wonderful book is the Bible. Compared with it, all other books are mere fragments. It is the one great commanding voice in comparison with which all other voices are but dying whispers. Let us close this section with two questions: "The Bible contains the mind of God, the state of man, the doom of the impentitent, and the eternal happiness of believers in Christ. Its doctrines are holy, its precepts binding, its histories true, its decisions immutable. Read it to be wise, believe it to be safe, practice it to be holy. It contains light to direct you, food to support you. It is the Christian's character. Christ is its subject, our good its design, and the glory of God its end." Study this book—"Supernatural in origin, inexpressible in value; infinite in scope; divine in authorship, though human in penmanship; regenerative in power; infallible in authority; personal in application; inspired in totality."

The Bible Book by Book

CHAPTER I

GENESIS

NOTE. "The Bible Book by Book" is intended as a guide to the study of the Bible itself. It is hoped not only that its contents will be mastered, but that the Bible itself will be read. To insure the study of both there are given at the beginning of each chapter suggested daily assignments. By following these a class may, in one year of nine months, master the contents of this book and read almost all of the Bible.

Lesson 1. Discussion of the text and Genesis, Chs. 1-4.
Lesson 2. Genesis, Chs. 5-11, with little emphasis on Genealogies in 10:1—11:26.
Lesson 3. Genesis, Chs. 12-19.
Lesson 4. Genesis, Chs. 20-27.
Lesson 5. Genesis, Chs. 28-36.
Lesson 6. Genesis, Chs. 37-45.
Lesson 7. Genesis, Chs. 46-50. Messages of the Book and Analysis.
Lesson 8. Review and discussion of topics "For Study and Discussion."

Name. The name means beginning, origin, or creation. The leading thought, therefore, is creation, and we should study it with a view to finding out everything, the beginning of which is recorded in it. Certainly we have the record of: (1) The beginning of the world which God created. (2) The beginning of man as the creature of God. (3) The beginning of sin, which entered the world through the disobedience of man. (4) The beginning of redemption, seen alike in the promises and types of the book and in the chosen family. (5) The beginning of condemnation, seen in the destruction and punishment of individuals, cities, and the world.

Purpose and Religious Importance. The chief purpose of the book is to write a religious history, showing how, after man had fallen into sin, God began to give him a religion and to unfold to him a plan of salvation. The germ of all the truth that is unfolded in the whole Scripture is found in Genesis, and to know this book well is to know God's plan for blessing sinful man. Above all, we learn about the nature and work of God, who is revealed as Creator, Preserver, Law-giver, Judge, and Merciful Sovereign. The religious interest dominates the whole book, as well as the whole Bible, and is uppermost even in the creation story. This religious purpose is seen in the fact that all but the chosen race are constantly dropped. It first gives the genealogy of Cain, then drops him and follows the line of Seth; first Ishmael is dropped and Isaac followed. Esau is given first and dropped while the story goes on to follow the line of Jacob.

Importance of Genesis to Science. Genesis is not a book of science and makes no attempt to explain many things that are the subject of investigation in the fields of geology, zoology, biology, botany, astronomy, archaeology, and anthropology. In fact, "Science does not come by revelation, but by observation, investigation, combination, conclusion," and hence Genesis leaves the unlimited fields of science free for investigation and discovery. But it does set out several facts which indicate the general plan of the universe and furnish a basis for scientific research. Among the more important things indicated are that: (1) There was a beginning of things. (2) Things did not come by chance. (3) There is a Creator who continues to take interest in and controls the universe. (4) There was orderly progress in creation from the less and more simple to the greater and more complex. (5) Everything else was brought into existence for man, who is the crowning work of creation.

General Importance. The importance of the book can not be overestimated. It alone tells us of the events that transpired before Moses. Without Genesis the Bible would be incomplete. We would know nothing of the origin of the universe and of man and sin; nothing of the flood and of the lives of Abraham, Isaac, Jacob, and Joseph—nothing of the beginning of the Hebrew race or of how God began to reveal Himself to man. Without it we could not understand the rest of the Bible, every part of which refers to the facts given here. It covers more than half of the time of all the Old Testament, and in it are the germs of all the truth unfolded in the rest of the Scriptures.

ANALYSIS

I. **Creation,** Chs. 1-2.
1. Creation in general, Ch. 1.
2. Creation of man in particular, Ch. 2.

II. **Fall,** Ch. 3.
1. Temptation, 1-5.
2. Fall, 6-8.
3. Lord's appearance, 9-13.
4. Curse, 14-21.
5. Exclusion from the Garden, 22-24.

III. **Flood,** Chs. 4-9.
1. Growth of sin through Cain, 4:1-24.
2. Genealogy of Noah, 4:25-5 end.
3. Building of the Ark, Ch. 6.
4. Occupying the Ark, Ch. 7.
5. Departure from the Ark, Ch. 8.
6. Covenant with Noah, Ch. 9.

IV. **Nations,** Chs. 10-11.
1. Basis of Nations, Noah's sons, Ch. 10. How?
2. Occasion of forming the nations, 11:1-9. Why?
3. Genealogy of Abraham and Shem, 11:10-32.

V. **Abraham,** 12:1-25:18.
1. Call and promise, Ch. 12.
2. Abraham and Lot, Chs. 13-14.
3. Covenant, 15:1-18:15.
4. Destruction of Sodom and Gomorrah, 18:16-19—end.
5. Lives at Gerar, Ch. 20.
6. Birth of Isaac, Ch. 21.
7. Sacrifice of Isaac, Ch. 22.
8. Death of Sarah, Ch. 23.
9. Marriage of Isaac, Ch. 24.
10. Death of Abraham and Ishmael, 25:1-18.

VI. Isaac, 25:19-36 end.

1. His two sons, 25:19—end.
2. Divine covenant, Ch. 26.
3. Jacob's deception, Ch. 27.
4. Jacob's flight into Haran, Ch. 28.
5. Jacob's marriage and prosperity, Chs. 29-30.
6. Jacob's return to Canaan, Chs. 31-35.
7. Generations of Esau. Ch. 36.

VII. Jacob, including Joseph, Chs. 37-50.

1. Jacob and Joseph, Chs. 37-45.
2. Sojourn in Egypt, Chs. 46-48.
3. Death of Jacob and Joseph, Chs. 49-50.

MESSAGES

NOTE. In each book an effort will be made to discover and state the chief spiritual lessons or messages that it contains. These lessons may not be taught in so many words, but may be such as one should imbibe from the atmosphere or spirit of the book—the lessons taught between the lines. These lessons should be thoroughly mastered.

(1) The near relation which man has to God, by whom and in whose image he was created, and who loves and cares for him and uses him in His world plans. (2) The intimate relation of men. Society is necessary but may be either a blessing or a curse, depending upon those with whom we have alliance. (3) The fundamental value of faith in the life and destiny of men. (a) It is the basis upon which God blesses us and accomplishes His purposes in us. (b) It is the means or instrument by which man is saved and accomplishes His tasks. (c) Without it, all in life is failure.

FOR STUDY AND DISCUSSION

NOTE. The topics included in this list found at the end of each book are intended to stimulate interest. They may be used as subjects for written themes or for oral discussion. In class work the teacher might at the beginning of the study of a given book assign these topics to the different members of the class so that when the study of the book is completed the information on each topic might be available for the whole class. This would facilitate discussions in review of the book.

(1) All that we may learn from this book concerning the nature and work of God. (2) The different things the origin of which this book tells. (a) Inanimate things,

(b) Plant life, (c) Animal life, (d) Human life, (e) Devices for comfort and safety, (f) Sin and varied efforts, (g) Various trades and manners of life, (h) Redemption, (i) Condemnation. (3) Worship as it appears in Genesis, its form and development. (4) The principal men of the book and the elements of weakness and strength in the character of each. The teacher may make a list and assign them for study to different pupils. (5) List the disappointments, family troubles and sorrows of Jacob, and study them in the light of his early deception and fraud. (6) The over-ruling divine providence seen in the career of Joseph, with the present day lessons from the incidents of his life. The Messianic promises, types and symbols of the entire book.

CHAPTER II

EXODUS

Lesson 9 Discussions of the text and Exodus, Chs. 1-5.
Lesson 10 Exodus 6:1-12:36.
Lesson 11 Exodus 12:37-19—end.
Lesson 12 Exodus, Chs. 20-26.
Lesson 13 Exodus, Chs. 27-34.
Lesson 14 Exodus, Chs. 35-40. Messages of the Book and Analysis.
Lesson 15 Review and discussion of topics "For Study and Discussion."

Name. The name Exodus means a going out or departure.

Subject. The subject and key-word of the book is redemption (3:7, 8; 12:13, etc.), particularly that half of redemption indicated by deliverance from an evil plight. It records the redemption of the chosen people out of Egyptian bondage, which becomes a type of all redemption in that it was accomplished (1) wholly through the power of God, (2) by means of a deliverer, (3) under the cover of blood.

Purpose. At this point Old Testament history changes from that of the family, given in individual biographies and family records, to that of the nation, chosen for the divine purposes. The divine will is no longer revealed to a few leaders but to the whole people. It begins with the cruel bondage of Israel in Egypt, traces the remarkable events of their deliverance, and ends with a complete establishment of the dispensation of the Law. The aim seems to be to give an account of the first stage in the fulfillment of the promises made by God to the Patriarchs with reference to the place and growth of the Israelites.

Contents. Two distinct sections are usually given by students; the historical, included in chapters 1-19, and the legislative, comprising chapters 20-40. The first section records the need of deliverance; the birth, training, and call of the deliverer; the contest with Pharaoh; the deliverance and march through the wilderness to Sinai. The second gives the consecration of the nation and the covenant upon which it was to become a nation. The laws were such as to cover all the needs of a primitive people, both moral, ceremonial, and civic, with directions for the establishment of the Priesthood and Sanctuary. For our purpose we have divided the contents into three sections with reference to the location of Israel, showing their experiences while in Egypt, while on the journey to Sinai, and while encamped at Sinai.

Exodus and Science. Scientific research has gone far toward establishing the truthfulness of the Exodus record, but has brought to light nothing that in any way discounts it. It has shown who the Pharaoh of the oppression and Exodus was (Rameses II, the Pharaoh of the oppression and Merenptah II, the Pharaoh of the Exodus), and has discovered Succoth. It has shown that writing was used long before the Exodus and has discovered documents written before that period. It has thus confirmed the condition of things narrated in the Bible.

ANALYSIS

I. **Israel in Egypt, 1:1-12:36.**
  1. The Bondage, Ch. 1.
  2. The Deliverer, Chs. 2-4.
  3. Preliminary contest with Pharaoh, 5:1-7:13.
  4. The Ten Plagues, 7:14-12:36.

II. **Israel Journeys to Sinai, 12:37-18 end.**
  1. The Exodus and Passover, 12:37-13:16.
  2. Journeying through Succoth to the Red Sea, 13:17-15:21.
  3. From the Red Sea to Sinai, 15:22-18 end.

III. Israel at Sinai, Chs. 19-40.

1. The people prepared, Ch. 19.
2. The Moral law, Ch. 20.
3. The Civil law, 21:1-23:18.
4. Covenant between Jehovah and Israel, 23:19-24 end.
5. Directions for building the tabernacle, Chs. 25-30.
   (1) The Ark, Mercy Seat, table of Shew-bread and candlestick, Ch. 25.
   (2) The curtains, boards, bars, veil and screen of the tabernacle, Ch. 26.
   (3) Altar of burnt offering court and lamps, Ch. 27.
   (4) Garments of the priests, Ch. 28.
   (5) Consecration of priests and daily offering, Ch. 29.
   (6) Altar of incense, atonement money, anointing oil and incense, Ch. 30.

6. The tabernacle prepared and dedicated, Chs. 31-40.
   (1) The covenant, given, broken, and renewed, Chs. 31-34.
   (2) Gifts and laborers for the tabernacle, Ch. 35.
   (3) The tabernacle constructed, Chs. 36-39.
   (4) Erection and dedication of the tabernacle, Ch. 40.

MESSAGES

1. **Some Revelations of God.** (1) That He is sovereign over all nature. (2) That He had power over Pharaoh; therefore power over all kings and nations. (2) That He had a right to choose Israel as His own peculiar people and no one could gainsay His election. (4) That He had ability to defend and care for His people and would do so.

2. **Some Thoughts as to Man.** (1) Redemption is necessary to his fellowship with God. (2) Redeemed people must worship and obey God. (3) Redemption and undefilement of life are secured by sacrifice and by the power of God.

FOR STUDY AND DISCUSSION

(1) The preparation of Israel and Moses for deliverance. (2) The Plagues. (3) The divisions of the Ten Command-

ments. (a) Those touching our relation to God, (b) Those touching our relation to men. (4) The different conferences between Jehovah and Moses, including Moses' prayer. (5) The current evils against which the civil laws were enacted and similar conditions of today. (6) The character of the different persons mentioned in the book: (a) Pharaoh, (b) Moses, (c) Aaron, (d) Jethro, (e) Magicians, (f) Amalek, etc. (7) The Messianic teachings of the book —here study (a) The Sacrifices, (b) the material, colors, etc., of The Tabernacle, (c) the smitten rock, (d) Moses and his family.

CHAPTER III

LEVITICUS

Lesson 16. Discussions of the text and Leviticus, Chs. 1-4.
Lesson 17. Leviticus, Chs. 5-10.
Lesson 18. Leviticus, Chs. 11-17.
Lesson 19. Leviticus, Chs. 18-23.
Lesson 20. Leviticus, Chs. 24-27, Messages of the Book and Analysis.
Lesson 21. Review and discussion of topics "For Study and Discussion."

Name. By the rabbis, it was called "The Law of the Priest" and "The Law of Offerings," but from the time of the Vulgate it has been called Leviticus, because it deals with the services of the sanctuary as administered by the Levites.

Connection with Former Books. In Genesis, man is left outside of the Garden, and the remedy for his ruin is seen in the promised seed. In Exodus, man is not only outside of Eden, but in bondage to an evil enemy and his escape from his bondage is shown to be in the blood of the lamb, which is shown to be sufficient to satisfy man's need and God's justice. In Leviticus there is given the place of sacrifice, as an atonement for sin, and it is shown that God accepted the sacrifice of the victim instead of the death of the sinner. It is a continuation of Exodus, containing the Sinaitic legislation from the time of the completion of the Tabernacle.

Contents. Except the brief historical sections found in chapters 8-10 and 24:10-14, it contains a system of laws, which may be divided into (1) Civil, (2) Sanitary, (3) Ceremonial, (4) Moral, and (5) Religious laws, emphasis being placed on moral and religious duties.

Purpose. (1) To show that God is holy and man is sinful. (2) To show how God can maintain His holiness and expose the sinfulness of man. (3) To show how a sinful people may approach a holy God. (4) To provide a manual of law and worship for Israel. (5) To make Israel a holy nation.

Key-Word. The key-word then is Holiness, which is found 87 times in the book, while in contrast with it, the words of sin and uncleanliness (in various forms) occur 194 times, showing the need of cleansing. On the other hand "blood" as a means of cleansing, occurs 89 times. The key verse is, I think, 19:2, though some prefer 10:10 as the best verse.

The Sacrifices, or Offerings. They may be divided in several ways, among which the most instructive is as follows: (1) *National Sacrifices,* which include: (a) Serial offerings, as the Passover, Cycle of Months, etc. (c) Offerings for the service of the Holy Place, as holy oil, precious incense, twelve loaves, etc. (2) *Official Sacrifices,* which include: (a) Those for the priests. (b) Those for princes and rulers. (c) Those for the holy women (Ex. 38:8; I Sam. 2:22). (3) *Personal Sacrifices,* including: (a) The blood offerings—peace offering, sin offering and trespass offering. (b) The bloodless offerings—the meat, or meal, offering.

Besides this general division, the offerings are divided into two kinds as follows: (1) *Sweet-Savor Offerings.* These are atoning in nature and represent Jesus as acceptable to God, not only because He does no sin, but because He does all good, upon which the sinner is presented to God in all the acceptableness of Christ. These offerings are: (a) The burnt offering, in which Christ is represented as willingly offering Himself without spot to God for our sins. (b) The meal offering, in which Christ's perfect humanity, tested and tried, is represented as the bread of His people. (c) The peace offering, representing Christ as our peace, giving us communion with God, and thanks. (2) *Non-Sweet-Savor Offerings.* These are perfect offerings, overlaid with human guilt. They are: (a) The sin offering, which is expiatory, substitutional and efficacious, referring more to sins against God, with little consideration of injury to man. (b) The trespass offering, which refers particularly to sins against man, which are also against God.

ANALYSIS

I. The Law of Sacrifices, 1:1-6:7.

1. Burnt offering, Ch. 1.
2. Meal offering, Ch. 2.
3. Peace offering, Ch. 3.
4. Sin offering, Ch. 4.
5. Trespass offering, 5:1-6:7.

II. Law of the Priests, 6:8-10 end.

1. Priests instructed concerning the offering, 6:8-7 end.
2. Aaron and his sons consecrated, Ch. 8.
3. The first offerings, Ch. 9.
4. Sin and death of the two sons of Aaron, the priest, Ch. 10.

III. Law of Purity, Chs. 11-22.

1. Pure food, animals to be eaten, Ch. 11.
2. Pure body and house, rules for cleansing, Chs. 12-15.
3. Pure nation, offering for sin on the day of atonement, Chs. 16-17.
4. Pure marriages, Ch. 18.
5. Pure morals, Chs. 19-20.
6. Pure priests, Chs. 21-22.

IV. Law of Feasts, Chs. 23-25.

1. Sacred feasts, Ch. 23.
2. Parenthesis, or interpolation, lamps of the Tabernacle, shewbread, the blasphemer, Ch. 24.
3. Sacred years, Ch. 25.

V. Special Laws, Chs. 26-27.

1. Blessing and cursing, Ch. 26.
2. Vows and tithes, Ch. 27.

MESSAGES

1. **Messages Concerning Sin.** The book everywhere implies the existence, the nature, and the awfulness of sin and shows it to be: (1) The lack of a knowledge of God; (2) The loss of communion with God; (3) Unlikeness to God; (4) Separation from God; (5) Wrong doing to God.

2. **Messages Concerning Redemption.** Redemption is seen throughout the book, all the main ideas of it being suggested as follows: (1) That it is founded on righteousness—God saves men, but not at the expense of righteousness. He must first be just. (2) That it is based on blood. The terrible record of blood and fire shows that redemption comes only through the shedding of blood, or the giving up of the life of the victim. (3) That it is in order to provide holiness. Redemption does not exempt one from holiness, but by it he is made holy. (4) That sacrifice is the basis, and the priesthood is the means, of access to God, the people are put on the ground of worship. (5) As to details it shows: (a) That it is by substitution—a truth seen in the sacrifices. (b) That it is by imputation—putting the sin on the victim. (c) That it is by death—the victim being slain. (d) That it is through love—the victim, being an animal, was innocent of sin, and was therefore given in love for the sinner. (6) In it all there is a revelation of Christ. He bears our sin and brings us into favor with God. Write Christ everywhere in the book—for every sacrifice, for every priest or garment or ceremony. He is all and in all in this book.

3. **Messages Concerning Fallen Human Nature.** We learn about human nature. (1) That it is an evil fountain and we must constantly watch everything that comes from it. (2) That it is not only defiled, but that it defiles whatever it touches. (3) That grace has made provision for this evil nature—that the atonement blood expiated it.

FOR STUDY AND DISCUSSION

(1) Make a list of the several offerings and become familiar with what is offered, how it is offered, the result to be attained in each case. (2) The laws: (a) For the consecration and purity of the priests (Chaps. 8-10 and 21-22). (b) Governing marriages (Chap. 18). (c) Concerning clean animals and what may be used for food (Chap. 11). (d) Governing vows and tithes (Chap. 27). (3) That sacrifice of the two goats and two birds: (a) The details of what is done with each goat and bird; (b) The lessons or truths typified by each goat and bird. (4) The name, occasion, purpose, time, and manner of observing each of the feasts. (5) Redemption as seen in Leviticus, (a) The place of the priest; (b) The place of substitution; (c) The place of imputation; (d) The place of sacrifice and blood in redemption. (6) The nature of sin as seen in Leviticus: (a) Its effect on man's nature; (b) Its effect on his relation to God.

CHAPTER IV

NUMBERS

Lesson 22. Discussions of the text and Numbers 1:47-54; 3:40-51, and Chs. 5-8.

Lesson 23. Numbers 9:1-10:10; Chs. 11-12, 12:17-14 end; Chs. 20-21.

Lesson 24. Numbers, Ch. 22-25; 27:12-23; Chs. 30-31; 35:6-34. Messages of the Book and Analysis.

Lesson 25. Review and discussion of the topics "For Study and Discussion."

Name. It is named from the two enumerations of the people, at Sinai, Chap. 1, and at Moab, Chap. 26.

Connection with Former Books. Numbers differs from the other books we have studied. Genesis tells of creation, Exodus of redemption, Leviticus of worship and fellowship, and Numbers of service and work. In Leviticus Israel is assigned a lesson and in Numbers she is getting that lesson. In this book, as in Exodus and Leviticus, Moses is the central figure.

Central Thought. The central thought of the book is *service.* This involves journeying and hence implies *walk* as a secondary thought. All the types and illustrations and experiences of the book bear upon this two-fold idea of service and walk.

Key-Phrase. The key-phrase of the book is "All that are able to go forth to war," which occurs fourteen times in the first chapter. There was fighting ahead, and all who could fight must muster in.

History Covered. The history covers a period of a little more than thirty-eight years (Num. 1:1; Deut. 1:3) and is a record: (1) Of how Israel marched to the border of Canaan, (2) Of how they wandered thirty-eight years in the wilderness while the old nation died and a new nation was trained in obedience to God, (3) Of how they finally returned to the border of the promised land.

Types and Illustrations of Jesus. This book is rich in illustrations and *types* that refer to Christ and the Christian experience and are recorded for our instruction and warning (1 Cor. 10:1-11). The following are the most important: (1) *The Nazarite.* He is an illustration of Christ as Holy, harmless and separate from sinners. He was to drink no wine which was a symbol of uncleanness and of natural joy. In this Jesus is prefigured as clean and deprived of ordinary rejoicing. His hair was not to be shorn. This was a woman's adornment. It showed that He would not depend on human strength and would be separate from others and from sin. (2) *The Blue Ribband.* This was the heavenly color and showed that God's people of all times should be heavenly in character. (3) *Aaron's Budding Rod.* This illustrates the resurrection of Jesus. Each head of a tribe laid up a dead rod and God caused Aaron's to live. It suggests how Christ our priest is alive from the dead. The authors of all other religions are dead; Christ also died, but God raised Him up and accepted Him as high priest. (4) *The Red Heifer.* Here is the representation of Christ as the ground of our cleansing. The slaying represents Christ's death; the seven-fold sprinkling of the blood suggests the complete, never-to-be-repeated putting away of our sins; the preservation of the ashes is a memorial of the sacrifice; the cleansing by sprinkling ashes mingled with water illustrates the work of the Holy Spirit and the word of God by which the sinner through the sacrifice of Jesus is cleansed. (5) *The Brazen Serpent.* This shows how Christ on the cross saves all who trust Him. (6) *The Cities of Refuge.* These show how Christ shelters us from judgment.

ANALYSIS

I. The Preparation of Sinai, 1:1-10:10.

1. The number and arrangement of the tribes, Chs. 1-2.
2. The choice and assignment of the Levites, Chs. 3-4.
3. Laws for the purity of the camp, Chs. 5-6.
4. Laws concerning the offerings for worship, Chs. 7-8.
5. Laws concerning the passover and cloud, 9:1-14.
6. Signals for marching and assembling, 9:15-10:10.

II. The Journey to Moab. 10:11-22:1.

1. From Sinai to Kadesh, 10:11-14 end.
2. From Kadesh to Kadesh (the wilderness wanderings), 15:1-20:21.
3. From Kadesh to Moab. 20:22-22:1.

III. The Sojourn at Moab, 22:2-36 end.

1. Balak and Balaam, 22:2-25 end.
2. The sum of the people, Ch. 26.
3. Joshua, Moses' successor, Ch. 27.
4. Feasts and offerings, Chs. 28-30.
5. Triumph over Midian, Ch. 31.
6. Two and a half tribes given land east of Jordan, Ch. 32.
7. Wilderness journeys enumerated, Ch. 33.
8. Divisions of Canaan and the cities of Refuge, Chs. 34-36.

MESSAGES

1. On Obedience. They were under law and under the immediate leadership of God, who punished them for every disobedience. This is a lesson for all nations.

2. On Doubts and Faith. Their doubts were manifested by complaints and murmurings; their lack of faith in God resulted in discontent. Their failure to see God gave them a narrow outlook and they lost their blessing and could not enter into Canaan because of unbelief.

3. On Comfort. This story has many comforting suggestions: (1) That though He punishes them, God deals patiently with His people and never forsakes them. (2) That He adapts His laws to meet the needs and conditions of His people (see the case of His dealing with the daughters of Zelophehad). (3) That He deals with His people with persistence and supernatural protection. (4) That God's promises for us are sufficient—that our final victory in Him is certain.

FOR STUDY AND DISCUSSION

(1) Make a list of the different times when God came to the relief of Israel, by providing guidance, protection, food, etc., and from them study God's wonderful resources in caring for His people. (2) Make a list of the different times and occasions when Israel or any individual sinned or rebelled against God or His leaders, and study the result in each case. (3) Make a list of the miracles of the book and give the facts about each. Show which were miracles of judgment and which miracles of mercy. (4) The story of the spies and the results of the mistake made as seen in all the future history of Israel. (5) The story of Balak and Balaam. (6) God's punishment of disobedient and sinful nations. (7) Doubt as a source of complaint and discontent.

CHAPTER V

DEUTERONOMY

Lesson 26. Discussions of the text and Deuteronomy, Chs. 1-4.

Lesson 27. Deuteronomy, Chs. 5-11.

Lesson 28. Deuteronomy, Chs. 12-20.

Lesson 29. Deuteronomy, Chs. 21-28.

Lesson 30. Deuteronomy, Chs. 29-34. Messages of the Book and Analysis.

Lesson 31. Review and discussion of topics "For Study and Discussion."

Name. The name comes from a Greek word which means a second or repeated law. It contains the last words of Moses, which were likely delivered during the last seven days of his life. It is not a mere repetition of the law, but rather an application of the law in view of the new conditions Israel would meet in Canaan, and because of their former disobedience.

Purpose. To lead Israel to obedience and to warn them against disobedience. The spirit and aim of the law is explained in such a way as to present both encouragement and warning.

Contents. It consists of three addresses of Moses, given on the plains of Moab at the close of the wilderness wanderings of Israel. They are soon to go over into the promised land and Moses gives them large sections of the law formerly given at Sinai, together with additions necessary to meet the new conditions. There is also the appointment of Joshua as Moses' successor and the farewell song of blessing of Moses and the record of his death.

Style. The style is warmer and more oratorical than that of former books. Its tone is more spiritual, and ethical, and its appeal is to "know God," "love God," and "obey God."

Occasion and Necessity of the Book. (1) A crisis had come in the life of Israel. The life of the people was to be changed from that of wandering in the wilderness to that of residence in cities and villages, and from dependence upon heavenly manna to the cultivation of the fields. Peace and righteousness would depend upon a strict observance of the laws. (2) They are to be tempted by a new religion of Canaan against which they must be put on guard. The most seductive forms of idolatry would be met everywhere and there would be great danger of yielding to it. Especially would they as farmers be tempted to worship Baal, who was thought to be the god of the farm and of crops. A poor crop would tempt them to worship him and bring upon themselves the displeasure of the Lord.

The Key-Word. "Thou shalt," so often repeated, as "thou shalt" and "shalt not." The key verses are 11:26-28.

ANALYSIS

I. Review of the Journeys, Chs. 1-4.

1. Place of their camp, 1:1-5.
2. Their history since leaving Egypt, 1:6-3 end.
3. Exhortation to obedience, 4:1-40.
4. Three cities of refuge on this side of Jordan, 4:41-49.

II. Review of the law, Chs. 5-26.

1. Historical and hortatory section, Chs. 5-11.
2. Laws of religion, 12:1-6:17.
3. Laws of political life, 16:18-20 end.
4. Laws of society and domestic relations, Chs. 21-26.

III. Future of Israel Foretold, Chs. 27-30.

1. Memorial tablets of stone, Ch. 27.
2. Blessing and cursing, Ch. 28.
3. Renewed covenant and Israel's future foretold, Chs. 29-30.

IV. Moses' Last Days, Chs. 31-34.
1. Charge to Joshua, Ch. 31.
2. Song of Moses, Ch. 32.
3. Blessing of Moses, Ch. 33.
4. Death of Moses, Ch. 34.

MESSAGES

(1) That the law of God is inflexible. It cannot be revoked or evaded, and is of universal operation. (2) That God's laws are the expression of His love. He governs man because He loves him and wants to prevent his ruin. (3) That man's obedience is the expression of his love. He obeys God because he loves Him and delights to promote His interests.

FOR STUDY AND DISCUSSION

(1) Make a list of the principal events of their past history of which Moses reminds Israel n Chapters 1-4, and find where in the previous books each incident is recorded. (2) From Chapter 11 make a list of reasons for obedience, the rewards of obedience, and the importance of the study of God's law. (3) The laws of blessing and cursing (Chaps. 27-28). Make a list of the curses, the sin, and the penalty, and a list of the blessings, indicating the blessing and that for which it is promised. (4) Make a list of the different countries or peoples concerning whom Israel was given commandment or warning. (5) Moses' farewell blessing on the several tribes (Chap. 33). Make a list of what shall come to each tribe. (6) The names, location, and purposes of the cities of refuge and the lessons for today to be drawn from them and their use. (7) The inflexibility of God's law.

CHAPTER VI

JOSHUA, JUDGES AND RUTH

Lesson 32. Discussion of the text on the Book of Joshua, and Joshua, Chs. 1-4.

Lesson 33. Joshua, Chs. 5-12.

Lesson 34. Joshua, Chs. 20-24, and Messages and Analysis of Joshua.

Lesson 35. Discussions of the text on the Book of Judges, and Judges, Chs. 1-4.

Lesson 36. Judges, Chs. 5-10.

Lesson 37. Judges, Chs. 11-16.

Lesson 38. Judges, Chs. 17-21, and Messages and Analysis of Judges.

Lesson 39. The entire book of Ruth—Analysis, Introductory discussions, Messages, and Scripture reading.

Lesson 40. Review of the three books and discussion of the topics "For Study and Discussion" of all three.

JOSHUA

Historical Books of the Old Testament. The twelve books, including those from Joshua to Esther, are called historical. They narrate the history of Israel from the entrance of Cannaan to the return from captivity, which is divided into three periods or epochs. (1) *The Independent Tribes.* This consists of the work of conquest of Canaan, and of the experiences of the Judges and is recorded in Joshua, Judges, and Ruth. (2) *The Kingdom of Israel.* (a) Its rise, I Sam. (b) Its glory, II Sam., I K. 1-11, I Chron. 11-29, II Chron. 1-9. (c) Its division and fall, I K. 12-22, II K. 1-25, II Chron. 10-36. (3) *The Return from Captivity.* Ezr., Neh. and Est.

Name. Taken from Joshua, the leading character, who may be described as a man of faith, courage, enthusiasm, fidelity to duty, and leadership.

Connection with Former Books. Joshua completes the story of the deliverance begun in Exodus. If Israel had not sinned in believing the evil spies and turning back into the wilderness, we would not have had the last twenty-one chapters of Numbers and the book of Deuteronomy. Joshua then would have followed the fifteenth chapter of Numbers, thus completing the story of God leading Israel out of Egypt into Canaan.

The Key-Word is "redemption," with the emphasis put upon possession, while redemption in Exodus put the stress upon deliverance. The two make full redemption which requires being "brought out" of evil and "brought into" the good.

Purpose of the Book. (1) To show how Israel was settled in Canaan according to the promise of God. (2) To show how, by the destruction of the Canaanites, God punishes a people for their sins. (3) To show that God's people are the final heirs on earth and that the wicked shall be finally dispossessed.

Some Typical and Spiritual Matters. (1) The conflict with Canaan. In the wilderness the conflict was with Amalek, which was an illustration of the never-ending conflict of the flesh or of the conflict between the "new man" and the "old man." In Canaan the conflict is typical of our struggle against principalities and powers and spiritual hosts in heavenly places, Eph. 6:10-18. (2) Crossing the Jordan is an illustration of our death to sin and resurrection with Christ. (3) The scarlet line illustrates our safety under Christ and His sacrifice. (4) The downfall of Jericho. This illustrates the spiritual victories we win in secret and by ways that seem foolish to men. (5) Joshua. Joshua is a type of Christ in that he leads his followers to victory over their enemies, and in that he is their advocate in time of defeat and in the way he leads them into a permanent home.

The War Against the Canaanites. Joshua's war of conquest against the Canaanites is one of the great wars of all time. Certainly no other was ever fought for a more noble purpose. It was a war fought on behalf of the whole world. On its issue depended the civil and religious liberty of the people. It gave to the world a new pattern of government as God's free nation, and a new conception of religion, free from idolatry, vice, and superstition. It established the Nation of Israel, through which came the Messiah to bless all nations.

ANALYSIS

I. **Conquest of Canaan,** Chs. 1-12.
   1. The preparation, Chs. 1-2.
   2. Crossing the Jordan, Chs. 3-4.
   3. Conquest of Jericho, Chs. 5-6.
   4. Conquest of South, Chs. 7-10.
   5. Conquest of North, Ch. 11.
   6. Summary, Ch. 12.

II. **Division of Lands,** Chs. 13-22.
   1. Territory of the different tribes, Chs. 13-19.
   2. Cities of Refuge, Ch. 20.
   3. Cities of the Levites, Ch. 21.
   4. Return of the Eastern Tribes, Ch. 22.

III. **Joshua's Last Counsel and Death,** Chs. 23-24.
   1. Exhortation to fidelity, Ch. 23.
   2. Farewell address and death, Ch. 24.

MESSAGES

1. **That God Is at War with Sin.** This is seen in several facts. (1) That after long probation He punished and cast

out the Canaanites because of their sins. (2) That He allowed Israel to be defeated at Ai because there was sin among them. (3) That God is still the enemy of sin, whether personal, social, civic, or national.

2. **That God Uses Instruments Against Sin.** (1) He uses men as far as they will suffice. (2) He uses the powers of nature. Examples of this are seen in the crossing of the Jordan, the falling of the walls of Jericho, and in the lengthening of the day.

3. **From the Conflict with the Canaanites.** Three truths are seen here: (1) That Israel's victory came through a leader and commander and not through a law-giver—through Joshua, not through Moses. So it is with a Christian. (2) That they entered Canaan through divine power and not by keeping the law. Likewise the Christian enters upon his present blessing—his present heavenly experience—not by works of the law, but by divine power. His future blessing will come in the same way. (3) the Christian, like Israel, must submit to God's standards of holiness and to His government.

FOR STUDY AND DISCUSSION

(1) The co-operation of the two and one-half tribes in the conquest of Canaan. (2) Make a list of the different battles of the book and indicate any in which Israel was defeated. (3) The story of the sin of Achan. Its results and his discovery and punishment. (4) The story of the Gibeonites, their stratagem and consequent embarrassment of Joshua. (5) Make a list of incidents and occurrences that show a miraculous element running through the narrative. (6) the story of Rahab, the harlot. (7) The place of prayer and worship in the narrative. Give instances. (8) Evidences found in the book that God hates sin.

JUDGES

Name and Character of the Book. The name is taken from the Judges whose deeds it records. The book is fragmentary and unchronological in its arrangement. The events recorded are largely local and tribal instead of national, but are of great value as showing the condition and character of the people.

Condition of the Nation. Israel was unorganized, and somewhat unsettled. They lacked moral energy and the spirit of obedience to Jehovah and were constantly falling into idolatry and then suffering at the hands of the heathen nations. This condition is summed up in the oft repeated words: "The children of Israel again did evil in the eyes of the Lord," and "the Lord sold them into the hand of the oppressor."

Contents. Judges records the conflict of the nation with the Canaanite people and with itself; the condition of the country, people, and times; and the faithfulness, righteousness, and mercy of God. It gives an account of "Seven apostasies, seven servitudes to the seven heathen nations, and seven deliverances." It furnishes an explanation of these "ups and downs," and is not merely a record of historical events but an interpretation of those events.

Work of the Judges. The Judges were raised up as occasion required and were tribesmen upon whom God laid the burden of apostate and oppressed Israel. They exercised judicial functions and led the armies of Israel against their enemies. They, therefore, asserted the nation's principles and upheld the cause of Jehovah. The name deliverer or savior used in some of the most ancient manuscripts describes their character and functions more accurately. But because individuals and clans in these turbulent times had differences that threatened to bring disastrous consequences they learned to refer such differences to these victorious leaders, a fact that caused them at a later time to be called Judges. As deliverers they were types of Christ.

The Key-Word is "Confusion" and the key-verse is "every man did that which was right in his own eyes" (17:6), which would certainly bring about a state of confusion.

Problems of the Times. Grave problems confronted Israel during this time. They were political problems, growing out of the isolated condition of the tribes; their tribal government, which lacked national unity; and the strength and oppression of the Canaanites. There were social problems, growing out of their adoption of Canaanite customs and manners of life and their intermarriage with the new people. There were religious problems, growing out of the satisfaction of their desires offered by Baal worship while the religion of Israel required purity. They were surrounded by hostile nations that sought to take for themselves the desirable districts of Palestine. All these conditions were such as to threaten the very life of the nation

ANALYSIS

I. From the Conquest to the Judges, 1:1-3:6.

II. The Judges and Their Work, 3:7-16 end.

1. Against Mesopotamia, 3:7-12.
2. Against Moab, 3:13-30.
3. Against Philistia, 3:31.
4. Against the Canaanites, Chs. 4-5.
5. Against the Midianites, Chs. 6-10.
6. Against the Amorites, Chs. 11-12.
7. Against the Philistines, Chs. 13-16.

III. The Idolatry of Micah, Chs. 17-18.

IV. The Crime of Gibea, Chs. 19-21.

MESSAGES

(1) Man must be governed as well as redeemed. (2) Instructions about national decay. Its cause is religious apostasy, its curse result in political and social disorder and chaos, its evidence is found in religious blindness, political folly, and social immorality. (3) Hope concerning God's government. His method is punishment, mercy, and deliverance. His deliverance is at the right time, with the right instrument, and with the best results. His deliverer must and will be found of God, but cannot be produced by us. (4) A warning and a hope. Beware, God will punish if we sin. Be encouraged. He is ever ready to pardon and will use us though we are weak instruments.

FOR STUDY AND DISCUSSION

(1) Learn the names of the Judges in order with the time each served, or the period of rest after his work had been accomplished. (2) The enemy each judge had to combat and what work was accomplished by each judge. (3) What elements of strength and of weakness are to be found in the character of each judge? (4) From the story of Gideon and Samson, point out New Testament truths. (5) From the story of Jephthah and Deborah gather lessons for practical life today. (6) Religious apostasy as a cause of national decay. (7) Political folly and social immorality as a sign of national decay. (8) The method of divine deliverance.

RUTH

This book, together with Judges, treats of the life of Israel from the death of Joshua to the rule of Eli. The name is taken from Ruth, the principal character. The other principal characters are Naomi and Boaz.

Contents. It is properly a continuation of Judges, showing the life of the time in its greatest simplicity. It is also especially important because it shows the lineage of David. Obed, the father of Jesse, who became father of David, was born of Ruth and Boaz her husband. Thus it is shown that Ruth connects herself with the whole history of Israel and forms a link in the genealogy of Christ.

Typical Matters. (1) Ruth is a type of Christ's Gentile bride and her experience is similar to that of any devout Christian. (2) Boaz, the rich Bethlehemite, accepting this strange woman, is an illustration of the redemptive work of Jesus.

The Key-Words are love and faith.

ANALYSIS

I. The Sojourn at Moab, 1:1-5.

II. The Return to Jerusalem, 1:6-22.

III. Ruth and Boaz, Chs. 2-4.

1. Gleaning the fields of Boaz, Ch. 2.
2. Ruth married to Boaz, Chs. 3-4.
   a. A bold act, Ch. 3.
   b. Redemption of Naomi's inheritance, 4:1-12.
   c. Becomes wife of Boaz, 4:13-17.
   d. Genealogy of David, 4:18-22.

Some one has said that Ch. 1 is Ruth deciding, Ch. 2 is Ruth serving, Ch. 3 is Ruth resting, Ch. 4 is Ruth rewarded.

MESSAGES

(1) Circumstances neither make nor destroy believers. This truth is seen from the two extremes of circumstances. Boaz had all opportunity and wealth, but was faithful and true; Ruth had no opportunity or childhood training, but nevertheless became glorious in character. We should learn here that God is our chief environment. (2) Faith is the

test or secret of discipleship. It overcomes all obstacles and gives us decision and courage. (3) The value of a trusting soul. Such an one will become an instrument of God. Ruth is put in the line of the faithful in the genealogy of Christ.

FOR STUDY AND DISCUSSION

(1) Each of the characters of the book; their strong and weak characteristics. (2) the Whole story of Ruth in comparison with the stories of Judges (Chaps. 17-21 to gain an estimate of the best and worst conditions of their social life.

CHAPTER VII

FIRST AND SECOND SAMUEL

Lesson 41. Discussions of text on First Samuel and Samuel, Chs. 1-7.

Lesson 42. I Samuel, Chs. 8-15.

Lesson 43. I Samuel, Chs. 16-23.

Lesson 44. I Samuel, Chs. 24-31, and Messages and Analysis of First Samuel.

Lesson 45. Discussion of the text on Second Samuel, and II Samuel, Chs. 1-7 and 9-10.

Lesson 46. II Samuel, Chs. 11-18.

Lesson 47. II Samuel, Chs. 19-24, and Messages and Analysis of Second Samuel.

Lesson 48. Review of both books and discussion of the topics "For Study and Discussion" on both.

FIRST SAMUEL

Name of the Two Books. The name is taken from the history of the life of Samuel recorded in the early part of this book. It means "asked of God." The two were formerly one book and called the "First Book of Kings," the two books of Kings being one book and called Second Kings. Samuel and Kings, form a continuous story, and give us a record of the rise, glory, and fall of the Jewish Monarchy.

Contents of First Samuel. This book begins with the story of Eli, the aged priest, judge and leader of the people. It records the birth and childhood of Samuel, who later becomes priest and prophet of the people. This story is scarcely less beautiful than that of Ruth. It describes the noble religious qualities of Samuel's mother which led him to his greatness, and shows how great a place godly women had in uplifting the Hebrew people. It would be difficult to find a more devout or loving mother or a more faithful or promising son. It tells of Saul's elevation to the throne and of his final downfall. Along with this is also given the growing power of David, who is to succeed Saul as king.

The Prophets. Samuel was not only both judge and priest and prophet, but as prophet he performed conspicuous services in several directions. Probably the most notable of all his work was the establishment of schools of prophets, which greatly dignified the work of the prophets. After this time, the prophet and not the priest was the medium of communication between God and His people.

Saul. As king, Saul began well and under favorable circumstances. He had wealth and influence; a fine physical appearance and a becoming modesty. He had the support of Samuel, the most influential man in the nation, and for a while was subservient to the will of God. He gave himself to military exploits and neglected the finer spiritual matters and soon made a complete break with Samuel, who represented the religious class—national class—and thereby lost the support of the best elements of the nation. He then became morose and melancholy and insanely jealous in conduct, and could not, therefore, understand the higher religious experiences that were necessary to him as a representative of Jehovah on the throne of Israel.

ANALYSIS

I. Career of Samuel, Chs. 1-7.

1. His birth and call, Chs. 1-3.
2. His conflict with the Philistines, Chs. 4-7.

II. Career of Saul to His Rejection, Chs. 8-15.

1. Chosen as King, Chs. 8-10.
2. Wars with Philistines, Chs. 11-14.
3. He is rejected, Ch. 15.

III. Career of Saul After His Rejection, Chs. 16-31.
1. While David is at his court, Chs. 16-20.
2. While David is a refugee in Judah, Chs. 21-26.
3. While David is a refugee in Philistia, Chs. 27-31.

MESSAGES

1. God Adapts His Reign to Conditions. While doing this He constantly advances His great plan. He lets them have a king, and appointed prophets who were closer to him than the king. The king was never a mediator between God and man, God choosing rather to speak to man through prophets. The kings themselves were compelled to go to the prophets for assistance and direction.

2. Man Co-operates in the Growing Purpose of God. This is seen in two ways: (1) The career of Saul showed the people the folly of wanting a king like other nations. (2) The career of David pointed out how God would give them an ideal king and gave them a higher conception of their great coming king. In both the failure and success of men God's purpose is set forward.

3. God's Victories Are Accomplished Through the Obedient and the Disobedient Alike. This is seen in the career of Samuel, Saul, and David. Note two facts concerning this: (1) That it is not God's victory that is determined by man's attitude toward Him, but man's place in that victory. Samuel and David were obedient and were used and saved. Saul was disobedient and was used but destroyed. (2) That man's attitude toward God does not affect His victory, but does determine man's destiny. Loyal souls aid the final victory and then share in the raptures of that victory, while rebellious souls aid the final victory and then share in the wrath of that victory.

FOR STUDY AND DISCUSSION

(1) The story of Eli and his sons. (2) The birth and call of Samuel. (3) the anointing of Saul. (4) The anointing

of David. (5) The evils of jealousy as seen in Saul. (6) The importance of respect for existing forms of government—see David's attitude toward Saul. (7) How a man's attitude towards God and His servants can make or mar his destiny. (8) Examples of how God uses both good and bad men in carrying forward His purposes.

SECOND SAMUEL

In this book there is given the story of the career of David while king of Israel. He was the strongest king Israel ever had and was characterized as a fine executive, a skilful soldier and was of a deeply religious disposition. He was not without his faults, but in spite of them developed a great empire. Taken as a whole, it is of profound, but also of painful, interest. Perhaps no other human soul ever had a more checkered record of sin and sorrow than is here given. There is true and genuine faith and also sin and lifelong punishment. There is stern chastening for iniquity, but also forgiveness, rest, peace, and strength in the God of his salvation (Psalm 51:14). With all of his faults he found favor with God and founded a royal line that ended in Christ, who is king over all. His closing years were full of trust in God and he approached the haven of eternal rest in the full enjoyment of the blessing of the everlasting covenant. It shows us a peaceful end of a troubled life.

ANALYSIS

I. David Made King and Reigning in Glory, Chs. 1-10.
II. David's Great Sin and Its Consequences, Chs. 11-18.
III. David Is Restored to His Throne, Chs. 19-20.
IV. An Appendix, Chs. 21-24.

MESSAGES

(1) Man's attitude toward God creates God's opportunity to make and use and bless him. David sinned, but was a

man after God's own heart. His heart *attitudes* were right. (2) God's attitude toward man creates man's opportunity to realize his highest possibilities. God is interested to help him. (3) "The finest triumph of man is God's triumph over him."

FOR STUDY AND DISCUSSION

(1) How David became King. (2) His victories in war. (3) His great sin and some of its consequences. (4) His kindness toward his enemies (see also his attitude toward Saul recorded in First Samuel). (5) The kindness of God is illustrated by the story of David's kindness to Mephibosheth, Chap. 9. (6) David's psalm of praise, Chaps. 22-23. (7) The different occasions when David showed a penitent spirit. (8) The great pestilence, Chap. 24.

CHAPTER VIII

FIRST AND SECOND KINGS

Lesson 49. Discussion of the text on First Kings and I Kings, Chs. 1-4.

Lesson 50. I Kings, Chs. 5-11.

Lesson 51. I Kings, Chs. 12-19.

Lesson 52. I Kings, Chs. 20-22. Messages and Analysis of First Kings and II Kings, Chs. 1-2.

Lesson 53. II Kings, Chs. 3-8.

Lesson 54. II Kings, Chs. 9-17.

Lesson 55. II Kings, Chs. 18-25, and Messages and Analysis of Second Kings.

Lesson 56. Review and discussion of topics "For Study and Discussion," both books.

Name. The two books of Kings were originally one book and form a continuous story. The name is taken from the Kings, whose deeds they narrate. It takes up the history of Israel where Second Samuel left off, and gives the account of the death of David, the reign of Solomon, the Divided Kingdom, and the Captivity.

Purpose. The political changes of Israel are given in order to show the religious condition. This is shown not only by what incidents he records, but by the way he passes judgment upon the several kings as good or bad. Everywhere there is a conflict between faith and unbelief, between the worship of Jehovah and the worship of Baal. We see wicked kings who introduce false worship and righteous kings who bring about reforms and try to overthrow false worship. Israel yields to evil and is finally cut off, but Judah repents and is restored to perpetuate the kingdom and to be the medium through which Jesus came.

The Kingdom of Solomon. Solomon began in glory, flourished a while and then ended in disgrace. He sacrificed the most sacred principles of the nation in order to form alliances with other nations. He attempted to concentrate all worship on Mount Moriah, probably hoping that in this way he might control all nations. He finally became a tyrant and robbed the people of their liberty. He showed great capacity to rule and thoroughly organized the kingdom into twelve divisions. He had a home policy of absolutism, a foreign policy of diplomacy, and a religious policy of centralization, all tending toward imperialism. He depended on military equipment and had other gods besides Jehovah, and thereby was led to his sad end.

The Two Kingdoms. This is a sad story of dissension and war and defeat. Israel, or the northern kingdom, was always jealous of Judah. It was by far the stronger, and possessed a much larger and more fertile land. There were nineteen kings, from Jeroboam to Hoshea, whose names and the number of years they reigned should be learned together with the amount of Scripture in the story of each. Judah, or the southern kingdom, had the religious capital of the nation with the temple as a center of Jehovah-Worship, and being more spiritual was always a little more faithful to the true worship. There were twenty kings, from Rehoboam to Zedekiah, whose lives with the number of years they reigned and the Scripture passages describing each, should be tabulated and learned.

The Captivity. It is made clear that the captivity is because of sin, God having spared them for a long time. (1) Israel was taken captive by the armies of the Assyrian Empire, whose capital was Nineveh. This marks the end of the northern tribe. (2) Judah was captured by the military forces of the Babylonian Empire, but after a period of seventy years, the people were restored to their own land.

Prophetic Activity. During these times the prophets were very active. The kings were for the most part wicked and were unwilling to submit to the divine will. This attitude and conduct on their part called forth frequent warnings and denunciations from the prophets. They spoke for Jehovah and tried to stir up the conscience of the nation. Both the non-writing and writing prophets were active, and did nearly all of their work during the period here set forth. They objected to the lustfulness, self-indulgence, and immorality of false worship which they constantly attacked. They saw that religion is a central factor of life, and freely condemned every type of evil conduct. They prophesied the fall of the nation and led the people to look for the glory of Israel through a coming Messiah.

ANALYSIS

NOTE. Two analyses are given—one continuous for the two books and showing the progress of the history through the two, the other for each book separately. Either may be used as the purpose of the student or class will be best served.

I. **The Reign of Solomon,** I Kings, Chs. 1-11.

1. His accession to the throne, I Kings, Chs. 1-4.
2. Building the temple, I Kings, Chs. 5-8.
3. His greatness and sin, I Kings, Chs. 9-11.

II. **The Divided Kingdom,** I Kings 12—II Kings 17.

1. Revolt and sin of the northern kingdom, I Kings, Chs. 12-16.
2. Career of Elijah, I Kings, Chs. 17-19.
3. Wickedness and death of Ahab, I Kings, 20-22.
4. Career of Elijah continued, II Kings, Chs. 1-2.
5. Career of Elisha, II Kings, Chs. 3-8.
6. Dynasty of Jehu, II Kings, Chs. 9-14.
7. Fall of Israel, II Kings, Chs. 15-17.

III. **The Kingdom of Judah,** II Kings, Chs. 18-25.

1. Reign of Hezekiah, Chs. 18-20.
2. Reign of Manasseh, Ch. 21.
3. Reign of Josiah, Chs. 22-23.
4. Fall of Judah, Chs. 24-25.

ANALYSIS OF FIRST KINGS

I. Reign of Solomon, I Kings, Chs. 1-11.
  1. His accession to the throne, Chs. 1-4.
  2. Building the temple, Chs. 5-8.
  3. His greatness and sin, Chs. 9-11.

II. Revolt and Sin of the Northern Kingdom, I Kings, Chs. 12-16.

III. Career of Elijah, I Kings, Chs. 17-19.

IV. Wickedness and death of Ahab, I Kings, Chs. 20-22.

ANALYSIS OF SECOND KINGS

I. Career of Elijah and Elisha, II Kings, Chs. 1-8.
  1. Career of Elijah continued, Chs. 1-2.
  2. Career of Elisha, Chs. 3-8.

II. From Jehu to the Fall of Israel, II Kings, Chs. 9-17.
  1. The dynasty of Jehu, Chs. 9-14.
  2. The fall of Israel, Chs. 15-17.

III. The Kingdom of Judah, II Kings, Chs. 18-25.
  1. Reign of Hezekiah, 18-20.
  2. Reign of Manasseh, Ch. 21.
  3. Reign of Josiah, Chs. 22-23.
  4. Fall of Judah, Chs. 24-25.

MESSAGES OF FIRST KINGS

1. Concerning the Failure of Human Governments. Here are two truths. (1) That all methods of men fail. This is true of Magnificence, Autocracy, Democracy, the different kings, etc. (2) That all national methods fail if God is left out of account.

2. Concerning the Unfailing Government of God. He carries on His government to His praise. This is done: (1) Through the utterance of truth (preaching) by the prophets. (2) By direct interference. This He does by the use of the forces of nature, such as famines, earthquakes, etc., and by raising up enemies and hostile armies.

MESSAGES OF SECOND KINGS

In addition to the lessons found in I Kings and as a sort of result of the condition found there, we may mention the following:

1. Concerning the Failure of Human Governments. Here we find: (1) The cause—a lost sense of Jehovah. See the idolatrous worship and the inability of the kings to see the working of God among them. (2) The manifestations—the loss of national ideals. Notice the low ideals of righteousness and their little concern for sin. (3) The helplessness—an insensitive conscience. Study their superficial reforms, their neglect of religious orders, etc. (4) The result—conquered, captured, cast away into national defeat.

2. Concerning the Victory of Divine Government. This is seen: (1) In His purpose. Study His promise to Abraham. (2) In His persistence. Note the repeated prophecies and warnings. (3) In His power. He will never let His people go, but will follow them till they are safe.

3. Concerning Man's Loss of a Vision of God. This leads to degraded ideals, deadened consciences, and defeated purposes.

FOR STUDY AND DISCUSSION

(1) Contrast the character of David with that of Solomon. Give the ideal elements and the defeats of each. Also compare them as rulers. (2) Contrast the character of Elijah with that of Elisha. Point out the elements of strength and weakness in each. Compare the great moral and religious truth taught by each as well as the great deeds performed by them. (3) Study this as the cradle of liberty. Note Elijah's resistance of tyrants and Ahab in the vineyard of Naboth. Look for the instances. (4) Consider

the place of prophets. Note their activity in the affairs of government. Glance through these books and make a list of all the prophets who are named and note the character of their message and the king or nation to whom each spoke. (5) Make a list of the kings of Israel and learn the story of Jeroboam I, Omri, Ahab, Jehu, Jeroboam II, and Hoshea. (6) Make a list of the kings of Judah and learn the principal events and the general character of the reign of Rehoboam, Jehoshaphat, Joash, Uzziah, Ahaz, Hezekiah, Manasseh, Josiah, and Zedekiah. (7) The fall of Judah.

CHAPTER IX

FIRST AND SECOND CHRONICLES

Lesson 57. Discussion of the text and I Chronicles, Chs. 13-17.

Lesson 58. I Chronicles, Chs. 22-29 and Messages of First Chronicles.

Lesson 59. II Chronicles, Chs. 10-20.

Lesson 60. II Chronicles, Chs. 21-28, Messages of Second Chronicles and the Analysis.

Name. The name Chronicles was given by Jerome. They were the "words of days" and the translators of the Septuagint named them the "things omitted." They were originally one book. Beginning with Adam the history of Israel is re-written down to the return of Judah from captivity.

Relation to Former Books. It covers the same field as all the others. Up to this time the books have fitted into one another and formed a continuous history. Here we double back and review the whole history, beginning with Adam, and coming down to the edict of Cyrus which permitted the exiled Jews to return to Jerusalem.

Religious Purpose of the Narratives. Several things show these books to have a religious purpose. (1) God's care of His people and His purpose to save them is given special emphasis. (2) The building of the temple is given much prominence. (3) The kings who served God and destroyed idols are given the most conspicuous place. (4) He follows the line of Judah, only mentioning Israel where it seemed necessary. In this way he was following the Messianic line through David. (5) The priestly spirit permeates these books instead of the prophetic element as in the earlier historical books. The aim, therefore, seems to be to teach rather than to narrate. This makes the book seem to be an ecclesiastical history. He seems to teach that virtue and vice, in private or in national affairs, will surely receive their dues—that God must be taken into account in the life of individuals and of nations.

ANALYSIS

NOTE. The analysis is continuous for the two books. If there is a desire to study them separately the first two divisions (I and II) may be used as the analysis for First Chronicles and the second two divisions for the analysis of Second Chronicles.

I. **The Genealogies,** I Chron., Chs. 1-9.

II. **The Reign of David,** I Chron., Chs. 10-29.
   1. Accession and great men, Chs. 10-12.
   2. Zeal for Jehovah's worship, Chs. 13-17.
   3. His victories, Chs. 18-20.
   4. Numbering the people, Ch. 21.
   5. Provision for the temple, Chs. 22-29.

III. **The Reign of Solomon,** II Chron., Chs. 1-9.
   1. Building the temple, Chs. 1-4.
   2. Dedicating the temple, Chs. 5-7.
   3. Solomon's greatness and wealth, Chs. 8-9.

IV. **Judah After the Revolt of the Ten Tribes,** II Chron., Chs. 10-36.
   1. Reign of Rehoboam, Chs. 10-12.
   2. Victory of Abijah, Ch. 13.
   3. Reign of Asa, Chs. 14-16.
   4. Reign of Jehoshaphat, Chs. 17-20.
   5. Seven kings and one queen, Chs. 21-28.
   6. Reign of Hezekiah, Chs. 29-32.
   7. Reign of Manasseh and Amon, Ch. 33.
   8. Reign of Josiah, Chs. 34-35.
   9. The captivity, Ch. 36.

MESSAGES OF FIRST CHRONICLES

1. God Must Be Considered in the Life of Nations. This fact is often overlooked, but is suggested: (1) By the fact that God is at work. By His choice and election some are excluded and others are accepted. Because of their obedience and the character it produces, some are received, and because of their disobedience others have all their rights and privileges cancelled. (2) By the fact that everything leads to the ultimate completion of God's purpose. The divine work is directed not only to the case of the Hebrews, but to all, and will accomplish His purpose. (3) By the fact that when God is left out there are no moral standards.

2. **The Test of Patriots.** Here is some sane advice. We should beware of the political sentiment or the politician that neglects God, attacks Him or opposes the national recognition of Him. The man who worships God is the true patriot, and the man who serves God can be trusted to serve his nation.

MESSAGES OF SECOND CHRONICLES

1. **Condemnation of Ritualism in National Life.** We must not only recognize God formally, but must fit our character and conduct to the symbol of our recognition of Him. The temple, which was the supreme inheritance of Solomon, was intended for an expression of Israel's relation to God, but its service became a mere form. Solomon's life failed to conform to its teachings. He followed sin and luxury and utterly failed.

2. **Neglect of Either the Form or the Fact of Religion Is to Fail in It.** Jeroboam substituted in Israel a false for a true form of religion, while Rehoboam kept the true form in Judah, but cared nothing for the fact. The influence of both alike led to irreligion and infidelity.

3. **All Reformation Must Begin in God's House.** (1) Some examples. Asa restored the altar which had been broken down and the vessels that had been desecrated. Jehoshaphat sent messengers everywhere to interpret the Scripture because there was general ignorance of God's

law, Joash restored God's house which had been destroyed. Hezekiah opened the doors of God's house which the people had closed because they had grown tired of mere formalism. Josiah carried forward his reformation by having the people use and conform to the law which he found and of which, because of its loss, they were ignorant. (2) Some conclusions: The temple then and the church now is the center and criterion of national life. The church should set the pace. No state, therefore, can establish a church, but the church, by giving right ideals, may establish and strengthen the state. But religion must not be formal. The church as the temple of God must be filled with the power of the Holy Spirit, and then it will move the world.

FOR STUDY AND DISCUSSION

(1) The men composing David's official family. (2) The different victories won by David. (3) The dedication of the temple, especially the prayer. (4) The wealth and follies of Solomon. (5) The Scripture and God's house as a means and source of all reformation. See: (a) Asa's restoration of the altar and its vessels; (b) Jehoshaphat's teaching the people God's law; (c) Joash and God's restored house; (d) The reforms of Josiah. (6) The reign of Manasseh. (7) The nature of the worship of Judah. (8) The captivity. (9) The value of true religion to a nation. (10) The evil results of idolatry.

CHAPTER X

EZRA, NEHEMIAH AND ESTHER

Lesson 61. Discussion of text on both books and Ezra, Chs. 1-6.

Lesson 62. Ezra, Chs. 7-10 and Messages. Analysis and topics "For Study and Discussion" on Ezra.

Lesson 63. Nehemiah, Chs. 1-7.

Lesson 64. Nehemiah, Chs. 8-13, and Messages, Analysis and topics "For Study and Discussion" on Nehemiah.

Lesson 65. Discussions of the text on Esther, Chs. 1-6.

Lesson 66. Esther, Chs. 7-10, and Messages, Analysis and topics "For Study and Discussion" on the book of Esther.

Lesson 67. Review studied lessons in Chs. IX and X.

EZRA AND NEHEMIAH

Name. Ezra and Nehemiah were formerly counted as one book and contain the account of the restoration of the exiles to Jerusalem and the re-establishment of their worship. They soon came to be called First and Second Ezra. Jerome first called the second book Nehemiah. Wyckliffe called them the first and second Esdras, and later they were called the books of Esdras, otherwise the Nehemiahs. The present names were first given in the Geneva Bible (1560). Ezra is so called from the author and principal character, the name meaning "help." Nehemiah is so called from the principal character, whose name means "Jehovah comforts."

Ezra is a very simple history, no other book of the Bible having fewer difficulties or obscurities. He makes little effort at direct teaching, but tells the story as simply as possible and lets it teach its own lessons. There is no effort to make the story continuous. He makes no mention of what took place during the nearly sixty years that intervened between chapters six and seven.

Nehemiah is a natural sequel to the book of Ezra. It tells the story of Nehemiah and is intended to describe the incidents connected with the rebuilding of the walls of Jerusalem. It is a personal narrative, the first two chapters giving us a purely personal sketch that describes the circumstances that led to his being the director of all the transactions connected with the renewal of the wall. Like Ezra it is a straightforward and simple story covering a short period, and like Ezra has no miraculous element. It is made clear, however, that Nehemiah was a strong man who thought for himself and expressed himself with great vigor.

Other Books. Three other books should be read in connection with this study. (1) The book of Esther, which relates to this time and should be read between chapters 6 and 7 of the book of Ezra. (2) The books of Haggai and Zechariah. These two prophets were associated with the first return of Zerubbabel and their words incited the Jews to complete the temple in spite of opposition.

Return from Captivity. The return consisted of three expeditions led respectively by Zerubbabel, Ezra, and Nehemiah. The time covered by these expeditions cannot be accurately calculated. Some think it may have been as many as 110 years. Others think it was 106 years, calculating 21 years for rebuilding the temple, 60 years as an interval before Ezra's reform, 13 years interval till the rebuilding of the wall, and 12 years interval with no details. The book ends abruptly and leaves the time uncertain, but it was probably not fewer than 90 years.

ANALYSIS OF EZRA

I. The Rebuilding of the Temple, Chs. 1-6.

1. The proclamation of Cyrus, Ch. 1.
2. Those who returned, Ch. 2.
3. The foundation laid, Ch. 3.
4. The work hindered, Ch. 4.
5. The work finished, Chs. 5-6.

II. The Reforms of Ezra, Chs. 7-10.

1. Ezra's journey, Chs. 7-8.
2. The confession of sin, Ch. 9.
3. The covenant to keep the law, Ch. 10.

MESSAGES OF EZRA

1. Concerning Jehovah's Instruments. Concerning those whom God uses in His work we learn two very interesting facts—that He uses some who are not of His own people, Israel, as Cyrus and Artaxerxes; that some are chosen from Israel, His chosen people, as Ezra, Zerubbabel, and Nehemiah.

2. Concerning Jehovah's Power. He employs it in two directions. First of all, it is constructive, being used to build up, inspire edicts, qualify workers, gather together His people, etc. But it is also destructive. It overcomes opposition.

FOR STUDY AND DISCUSSION OF EZRA

(1) The traits of character displayed by Ezra. (2) The reforms of Ezra. (a) What are they? (b) Parallel conditions of today. (3) The adversaries of Judah. (a) Who were they? (b) The nature of their opposition. (4) The decree of Cyrus. (5) The expedition of Zerubbabel and Ezra. (6) Ezra's commission and the king's orders, Chap. 7. (7) God's use of friends and enemies in forwarding His purposes.

ANALYSIS OF NEHEMIAH

I. The Rebuilding of the Wall, Chs. 1-7.

1. Nehemiah permitted to go to Jerusalem, Chs. 1-2.
2. The work on the walls and its hindrance, Chs. 3-7.

II. The Covenant to Keep the Law, Chs. 8-10.

1. The law read, Ch. 8.
2. Confession made, Ch. 9.
3. The covenant made, Ch. 10.

III. The Walls Dedicated and Nehemiah's Reforms, Chs. 11-13.

1. Those who dwelt in the city, 11:1-12:26.
2. The walls dedicated, 12:27-47.
3. Evils corrected, Ch. 13.

MESSAGES OF NEHEMIAH

1. From Nehemiah's Attitude Toward God's Cause. Here are three things commendable: (1) He had a concern for God's cause. This is indicated by his earnest inquiry, by his deep sorrow for Jerusalem, etc. (2) He had confidence in God's cause and could pray for it and plead with heathen kings for it. (3) He co-operated in God's cause and actively fitted into the divine plan and works.

2. From Nehemiah's Activity. Here again are three things: (1) He was cautious. His secret visit to the walls and his division and distribution of the laborers are good illustrations. (2) He was courageous. He stood alone as leader of the enterprise and worked on, refusing to be frightened away by enemies. (3) He was uncompromising. He would neither compromise with outsiders, such as Sanballat, nor with those among his own people, such as the nobles.

3. From Nehemiah's Life of Faith. He trusted God fully, was clearly conscious of His presence and aid, and performed all his work in the interest of God's cause.

FOR STUDY AND DISCUSSION OF NEHEMIAH

(1) Point out elements of strength in the character and work of Nehemiah. (2) The greatness and difficulty of Nehemiah's task. (a) The rubbish; (b) the size and length of the wall; (c) the strength of their enemies. (3) The reforms of Nehemiah; (a) religious; (b) moral; (c) political. (4) The public meeting and new festival, Chap. 8. (5) The covenant, Chaps. 9-10. (6) The re-peopling of Jerusalem, Chaps. 11-12.

ESTHER

The Name of this book is taken from its principal character, a Jewish maiden who became queen of a Persian king. It is given us to explain the origin of the feast of Purim and to show the work of providence for God's people. It relates an episode in Jewish history that threatened the destruction of the entire nation.

Time. The events narrated are thought to have occurred about 56 years after the first return of Zerubbabel in 536 B. C. The King then would be Xerxes the Great, and the drunken feast may have been preparatory to the invasion of Greece in the third year of his reign.

Connection with Other Books. There is no connection between Esther and the other books of the Bible. While it is a story of the time when the Jews were returning to Jerusalem, and very likely should come between the first and second return, and therefore between the sixth and seventh chapters of Ezra, the incident stands alone. It is distinct and separate from the rest of Jewish history, not being connected with anything that preceded or followed. There is no mention of Palestine, or Jerusalem, or the temple, or the provisions of the law, nor any reference to any facts of Jewish history except the captivity under Nebuchadnezzar and the dispersion of the Jews throughout the Persian empire. But without it we would lose much of our knowledge of that period.

The Story. While Esther stands out as the principal character, the whole story turns on the refusal of Mordecai to bow down to Haman, which would have been to show him divine honor. He did not hate Haman, but, as a Jew, could not worship any other than God and he dared to stand for principle at the risk of his life.

The Name of God. One of the peculiarities of the book is that it nowhere mentions the name of God, or makes any reference to Him. This may be because His name was held secret and sacred at that time. However, God's power and His care of His people are everywhere implied in the book.

ANALYSIS

I. Esther Made Queen, Chs. 1-2.

1. Queen Vashti dethroned, Ch. 1.
2. Esther made Queen, Ch. 2.

II. Haman's Plot and Its Defeat, Chs. 3-8.

1. Haman plots the destruction of the Jews, Ch. 3.
2. The Jews' mourning and Mordecai's plea to Esther, Ch. 4.
3. Esther banquets Haman and the king, Ch. 5.
4. Mordecai highly honored for former service and faith, Ch. 6.
5. Esther's plea granted and Haman hanged, Ch. 7.
6. The Jews allowed defense and Mordecai advanced, Ch. 8.

III. The Jews' Deliverance, Chs. 9-10.

1. Their enemies slain, 9:1-16.
2. A memorial feast is established, 9:17-32.
3. Mordecai made great, Ch. 10.

MESSAGES OF ESTHER

(1) Three great truths—There is a God, God acts in providence, and God touches life at every point. (2) Three great duties—We must reckon with God, we must trust God, and we must act for and in harmony with God. (3) Three lessons in God's work in providence—It is hidden, but all-inclusive. It displays perfect righteousness, perfect knowledge, and perfect power. It results in confidence and courage for believers, in fear and punishment for the disobedient, and in progress and blessing in all history.

FOR STUDY AND DISCUSSION

(1) The character of the king, Vashti, Mordecai, Esther, and Haman. (2) Mordecai's plea to Esther. (3) The honor

of Mordecai and humiliation of Haman, Chap. 6. (4) The destruction of their enemies. (5) The feast of Purim, 9:17-32. (6) Truth about God seen in this book. (7) Why not name the book Mordecai or Vashti—are they not as heroic as Esther? (8) The race devotion of the Jews, then and now. (9) Persian life as seen in the book.

CHAPTER XI

JOB, PSALMS, AND PROVERBS

Lesson 68. Discussions, Messages, Analysis and Chs. 1, 2, 31, and 42 of Job.

Lesson 69. Discussions on the book of Psalms, Analysis and hymns in groups (1), (2) and (3) on subject of the Psalms in the Introductory Discussions.

Lesson 70. Hymns in groups (4), (5) and (6) on subjects of Psalms in the Introductory Discussions and the Messages of the book.

Lesson 71. Analysis of Proverbs, Introductory Discussions, and Chs. 1-9.

Lesson 72. Proverbs, Chs. 25-31, Messages of the book, and topics "For Study and Discussion" based on portions of the book studied.

JOB

The Name, Job, is taken from its chief character, or hero, which means *Persecuted.* It stands alone, being one of the so-called wisdom books of the Bible, but has no connection with any of the other Biblical books.

Date. Neither the date nor the author can be determined with certainty. I incline to the theory of the Job authorship. It has to do with events and relates to people and customs that belong to the patriarchal age—to the age of Abraham or earlier. It nowhere alludes to the Mosaic law or the history of Israel. One can hardly believe that it was written after the giving of the law and deliverance out of Egypt and into Canaan. A writer of those times would hardly have remained silent on those great matters.

Literary Characteristics. Chapters one and two and parts of chapter forty-two are prose. All the rest is poetry. The different speakers may have been real speakers, or characters created by one writer to make the story. There is, however, little doubt that the story is founded on historical facts.

The Problems of the Book. This book raises several great questions, that are common to the race, and directly or indirectly discusses them. Among those questions the following are the most important: (1) Is there any goodness without reward? "Doth Job serve God for naught"? (2) Why do the righteous suffer and why does sin go unpunished? (3) Does God really care for and protect His people who fear Him? (4) Are adversity and affliction a sign that the sufferer is wicked? (5) Is God a God of pity and mercy? There are presented five solutions of the problem of suffering: (1) The solution of chapters one and two —that it is a test of character and abundantly rewarded when rightly endured; (2) The solution of Job's friends— that it is always a punishment for sin; (3) The solution of Elihu—that it is closely connected with sin, sent as the voice of God to call us back to Him; (4) The solution of Job who never seems fully settled, on one occasion looking to the future life for a solution (19:25-37) and later pleading a chance to present his case to God (Chaps. 29-31). (5) The solution of God—that while there is mystery in both good and evil, man's attitude should be one of submission and faith.

The Argument. The argument proceeds as follows: (1) There is a conference between God and Satan, and the consequent affliction of Job. (2) The first cycle of discussion with his three friends in which they charge Job with sin and he denies the charge. (3) The second cycle of discussion. In this Job's friends argue that his claim of innocence is a further evidence of his guilt and impending danger. (4) The third cycle. In this cycle Job's friends argue that his afflictions are just the kind that would come to one who yielded to temptations such as those to which he is subject. In each of the three cycles of discussion with his friends, Eliphaz, Bildad, and Zophar, each argues with Job except that Zophar remains silent in the third cycle. They speak in the same order each time. (5) Elihu shows how Job accuses God wrongly while vindicating himself and asserts that suffering instructs us in righteousness and prevents us from sinning. (6) God intervenes and in two addresses instructs Job. In the first address, Job is shown the creative power of the Almighty and his own folly in answering God whom animals by instinct fear. In the second address, Job is shown that one should know how to rule the world and correct its evils before one complains or accuses God as to the way He rules it. (7) Job prays and is restored.

Purpose. The purpose of the book, then, is to justify the wisdom and goodness of God in matters of human suffering, and especially to show that all suffering is not punitive.

Job's Temptation. Job's temptation came by stages and consisted largely in a series of losses as follows: (1) His property, (2) his children, (3) his health, (4) his wife's confidence—she would have him curse God and die, (5) his friends who now think him a sinner, (6) the joy of life—he cursed the day of his birth, (7) his confidence in the goodness of God—he said to God, "Why hast thou set me as a mark for thee?" In his reply to Elihu he doubts the justice if not the very existence of God. In all this he is stripped of everything earthly that would afford pleasure. A more abject picture could hardly be painted.

ANALYSIS

I. Job's Wealth and Affliction, Chs. 1-2.

II. The Discussion of Job and His Three Friends, Chs. 3-31.

1. **The first cycle, Chs. 3-14.**
2. **The second cycle, Chs. 15-21.**
3. **The third cycle, Chs. 22-31.**

III. The Speech of Elihu, Chs. 32-37.

IV. The Addresses of God, Chs. 38-41.

1. The first address, Chs. 38-39.
2. The second address, Chs. 40-41.

V. Job's Restoration, Ch. 42.

MESSAGES OF JOB

The story of Job brings to us distinct messages concerning the needs and longings of sinful men. They relate to such needs and inquiries as could never be met till Jesus came to fill every need and answer every longing of the heart of man. (1) There is a cry for a daysman or mediator, one that might "put his hand upon both of us." (2) There was longing for light on the future—"If a man die shall he live again?" (3) There was need for one to argue or plead his cause. God must do that—Christ provides for it. "He is not a man as I am that I should answer him." (4) There is need of a redeemer or vindicator. "I know that my redeemer (vindicator) liveth." (5) We must have a judge, one before whom our vindicator may go and make his arguments and plead our cause. (6) We need a book of indictment to show the charges against us. The Bible is the book which God wrote, 31:35. (7) There is need of a vision of God, such as will give us a sense of God's righteousness, and of man's worth, such as would lead to repentance.

FOR STUDY AND DISCUSSION

(1) The personality and malice of Satan. Point out his false accusations against Job and God, also the signs of his power. (2) Concerning man, look for evidence of: (a) The folly of self-righteousness; (b) the vileness of the most perfect man in God's sight; (c) the impossibility of man, by wisdom, apart from grace, finding God. (3) Concerning

God, gather evidence of His wisdom, perfection, and goodness. (4) Job's disappointment in his friends. (5) Elements of truth and falsehood in the theory of Job's friends. (6) Job's despair of the present, his view of Sheol, and his view of the future. Does he believe in a future life or think all ends with the grave? Does the book really explain why the righteous are allowed to suffer? (7) Make a list of the striking passages especially worthy of remembering.

PSALMS

Name. The Hebrew word means praises or hymns, while the Greek word means psalms. It may be called the "Hebrew Prayer and Praise Book." The prevailing note is one of praise, though some are sad and plaintive, while others are philosophical.

Authors. Of the 150 Psalms, there is no means of determining the authorship of 50. The authors named for others are David, Asaph, the sons of Koran, Heman, Ethan, Moses, and Solomon. Of the 100 whose authorship is indicated, David is credited with 73, and in the New Testament he alone is referred to as the author of them, Luke 24:44.

Relation to the Other Old Testament Books. It has been called the heart of the entire Bible, but its relation to the Old Testament is especially intimate. All divine manifestations are viewed in regard to their bearing on the inner experience. History is interpreted in the light of a passion for truth and righteousness and as showing forth the nearness of our relation to God.

Subjects of the Psalms. It is very difficult to make any sort of classification of the Psalms and any classification is open to criticism. For this reason many groupings have been suggested. The following, taken from different sources, may be of help: (1) Hymns of praise, 8, 18, 19,

104, 145, 147, etc. (2) National hymns, 105, 106, 114, etc. (3) Temple hymns, or hymns for public worship, 15, 24, 87, etc. (4) Hymns relating to trial and calamity, 9, 22, 55, 56, 109, etc. (5) Messianic Psalms, 2, 16, 40, 72, 110, etc. (6) Hymns of general religious character, 89, 90, 91, 121, 127, etc.

The following classification has been given in the hope of suggesting the most prominent religious characteristics of Psalms: (1) Those that recognize the one infinite, all-wise, and omnipresent God. (2) Those that recognize the universality of His love and providence and goodness. (3) Those showing abhorrence of all idols and the rejection of all subordinate deities. (4) Those giving prophetic glimpses of the Divine Son and of His redeeming work on earth. (5) Those showing the terrible nature of sin, the divine hatred of it and judgment of God upon sinners. (6) Those teaching the doctrine of forgiveness, divine mercy, and the duty of repentance. (7) Those emphasizing the beauty of holiness, the importance of faith, and the soul's privilege of communion with God.

This variety on the one hand and unity on the other has given the book a unique place in the religious life of individual Christians and churches. It has gripped the heart of all Christendom and molds the affections, sustains the hopes, and purifies the faith of all believers. It matches all of our feelings whether of ambition, sorrow, confession, joy, or thanksgiving.

ANALYSIS

1. **Davidic Psalms, 1-41.**

   These are not only ascribed to him, but reflect much of his life and faith.

2. **Historical Psalms, 42-72.**

   These are ascribed to several authors, those of the sons of Korah being prominent, and are especially full of historical facts.

3. **Liturgical or Ritualistic Psalms, 73-89.**

   Most of them are ascribed to Asaph and, besides being specially prescribed for worship, they are strongly historical.

4. **Other Pre-Captivity Psalms, 90-106.**

   Ten are anonymous, one is Moses' (Ps. 90), and the rest David's. They reflect much of the pre-captivity sentiment and history.

5. **Psalms of the Captivity and Return, 107-150.**

   Matters pertaining to the captivity and the return to Jerusalem.

MESSAGES OF PSALMS

1. Concerning Man's Attitude in Worship. Here are three words of value: (1) He must be submissive. This is man's response to God's sovereignty, which requires reverence and obedience. (2) He must trust God. This is man's response to God's power and requires honesty and courage. (3) He must be joyful. This is man's response to God's grace and requires penitence and adoration.

2. Concerning the Persons in Worship. They are two, (1) God, who calls man to worship and involves revelation. Moreover, God is true and faithful and deals in love. (2) Man, who approaches God, lays bare his soul, receives God's gifts and offers praise.

FOR STUDY AND DISCUSSION

(1) On what occasion were the following Psalms probably composed: (a) Psalm 3 (II Sam. 15); (b) Psalm 24 (II Sam. 6:12-17); (c) Psalm 56 (I Sam. 21:10-15); (d) Psalms 75 and 76 (II Kings 19:32-37); (e) Psalm 109 (I Sam. 22:9-23); (f) Psalm 74 (II Kings 25:2-18); (g) Psalm 60 (I Chron. 18:11-13). (2) What are the subjects of Psalms 23, 84, 103, 133, and 137? (3) What doctrines of the divine character are taught in each of the following Psalms: 8, 19, 33, 46, 93, 115, and 139?

PROVERBS

Practical Value of the Book of Proverbs. The proverbs emphasize the external religious life. They teach how to practice religion and overcome the daily temptations. They express a belief in God and His rule over the universe and, therefore, seek to make His religion the controlling motive in life and conduct. They breathe a profound religious conception, but put most stress upon the doing of religion in all the relations of life. Davison says: "For the writers of Proverbs religion means good sense, religion means mastery of affairs, religion means strength and manliness and success, religion means a well-furnished intellect employing the best means to accomplish the highest ends." This statement is correct as far as the side of duty emphasized is concerned. Underneath all these teachings, however, there was a firm belief in the existence of God and in His rule over the world. Everything rests on a religious basis (3:5-7; 16:3, 6, 9; 23:17). There are passages that refer to national life and proper relation to government (14:34, 35; 16:12-15); to domestic relations and happiness (6:20-22; 18:22; 3:10-31); to the relation of men to their fellows (11:1; 14:21; 17:5); to everyday conduct (10:4; 11:28; 12:10; 14:3).

Nature of Proverbs. (1) There is a voice of wisdom which speaks words of wisdom, understanding, knowledge, prudence, subtlety, instruction, discretion, and the fear of Jehovah, and furnishes us with good advice for every condition of life. (2) There is a voice of folly, which speaks words of folly, simplicity, stupidity, ignorance, brutishness, and villainy, and lifts her voice wherever wisdom speaks. (3) Wisdom is contrasted with folly, which often issues in simplicity and scorning. (4) Wisdom is personified, as if it were God speaking about the practical, moral, intellectual, and religious duties of men. (5) Since it is a part of all the Scriptures, Christ finds Himself in the book, Luke 24:27. And, if Christ be substituted for wisdom, where it is found, a new and wonderful power will be seen in the book.

Scheme of the Considerations Found in Proverbs. The first sphere—the home, father, and mother and children are the persons involved, 1:8-9 and Chaps. 2-7. Key word here is "my son." The second sphere—friendship, companions is the important word for the lessons here. They must be wisely chosen, 1:10-19. The third sphere—the world beyond.

ANALYSIS

I. **The Praise of Wisdom,** Chs. 1-9. **This is shown by contrast with folly.**

1. The design and some fundamental maxims, 1:1-19.
2. Wisdom's warnings, 1:20 end.
3. Wisdom will reveal God and righteousness and save one from wicked men and strange women, Ch. 2.
4. Description of the life of wisdom, Ch. 3.
5. Wisdom the best way, Ch. 4.
6. The strange woman, Ch. 5.
7. Against various evils, Ch. 6.
8. Wisdom's warnings against the seductions of an adulterous woman, Ch. 7.
9. Wisdom makes an appeal, Ch. 8.
10. Wisdom gives her invitations, Ch. 9.

II. **Practical Proverbs of Solomon,** 10:1-22:16.
These are separate and cannot be classified.

III. **Words of the Wise,** 22:17-24 end.

Sometimes called commendations of justice. There are several authors, but no common topic.

IV. **Proverbs of Solomon, Copied by the Scribes of Hezekiah,** Chs. 25-29.

V. **Words of Agur,** Ch. 30.

From one who has tried "to find out God unto perfection and found the task above him."

VI. **Words of Lemuel,** Ch. 31.

1. The duty of kings, 1-9.
2. The praise of a virtuous woman or good wife, 10-31.

MESSAGES OF PROVERBS

It is most difficult to draw from this book any special lessons. The book is fundamentally didactic and as a result the content constitutes its message. Among the outstanding lessons, however, the following are vital: (1) That God is all-wise. This is probably the greatest teaching of the book. (2) That man's greatest wisdom is in fearing God. The very fact of His wisdom suggests this. (3) The youth is not to stay out of the crowd and out of busy life, but is not to enter them forgetful of God. (4) The value of young people taking the advice of their parents. (5) The fundamental danger of bad companions.

FOR STUDY AND DISCUSSION

(1) Collect passages that tell of the rewards of virtue and piety. (2) Cite passages that show the evils of sloth or indolence, of wine-drinking and drunkenness, of tale-bearing, of family contentions. (3) Make a list of the chief thoughts of the book concerning God, man, and other great religious teachings of our day. (4) What is said of a man who rules his own spirit, of a good name, of obedience to parents, of fitly spoken words, of a beautiful woman who lacks discretion, of a liberal soul, of a false balance, of a soft answer, of a wise son. Find where the answers are found. (5) The peril of following an unchaste love (woman), Chapter 5. (6) Folly of yielding to the wiles of an harlot, Chapter 7. (7) The description of a worthy woman, 31:10 end.

CHAPTER XII

ECCLESIASTES AND SONG OF SOLOMON

Lesson 73. Analysis, Introductory Discussions and Chs. 1-6 of Ecclesiastes.

Lesson 74. Ecclesiastes, Ch. 7-12, Messages of the book and topics "For Study and Discussion."

Lesson 75. The Son of Solomon—Analysis, Introductory Discussions and the reading of the book in Scripture.

Lesson 76. Reading of Chs. X and XII, with a discussion of the topics "For Study and Discussion" involved in the sections of the poetical books studied.

ECCLESIASTES

Name. The Hebrew word means *preacher* and refers to or signifies one who calls together and addresses assemblies.

The Personal or Human Element. Such expressions as "I perceived," "I said in my heart," "I saw," etc., indicate that it is not the will of God that is developed, but a man is telling of his own ventures and utter failure. It is what he has seen and experienced.

The General View or Key-phrase is "under the sun," with the sad refrain, "vanity of vanities, all is vanity," and shows how a man under the best possible conditions sought for joy and peace, trying at its best every human resource. He had the best that could be gotten, from human wisdom, from wealth, from worldly pleasure, from worldly honor, only to find that all was "vanity and vexation of spirit." It was what a man, with the knowledge of a holy God and that He will bring all into judgment, has learned of the emptiness of things "under the sun" and of the whole duty of man to "fear God and keep His commandments."

Purpose of the Book. The purpose, then, is not to express the doubts or skepticism of the writer, not to record the complaining of a bitter spirit. It is not the story of a pessimist or of an evil man turned moralist. But it is intended to show that, if one should realize all the aims, hopes and aspirations of life, they would not bring satisfaction to the heart. His experience is used to show the result of successful worldliness and self-gratification in contrast with the outcome of the higher wisdom of the Godly life. We are shown that man was not made for this world alone and not for selfish achievement or gratification, but to fulfill some great plan of God for him which he will accomplish through obedience and Divine service. He is conscious of a divine order in the world and realizes that a man who fears God has an advantage over all others.

ANALYSIS

I. **The Vanities of Life,** Chs. 1-4, seen in both experience and observation.
   1. The Vanity of what he has experienced, Chs. 1-2.
   2. The Vanity of what he has observed, Chs. 3-4.

II. **Practical Wisdom,** Chs. 5-7.
   1. Some prudential maxims, Ch. 5.
   2. Some vanities, Ch. 6.
   3. The best way to get along in life, Chs. 7.

III. **Rules for a Happy Life,** Chs. 8-11.

IV. **Conclusion of the Whole Matter,** Ch. 12.

MESSAGES OF ECCLESIASTES

1. Concerning Conviction and Conduct. From these studies we learn that conviction and conduct according as they are related have much to do with character. (1) That conviction affects character through conduct. (2) That conduct untrue to conviction destroys both character and conscience. (3) That conduct guided by conviction makes and fulfills character. (4) That conviction must be right and conduct must be in harmony with it.

2. **Concerning God in Our Life.** Here are the two sides of it. To leave God out of one's life is to lose the key to success in life. To enthrone God in one's life is to make life a victory.

FOR STUDY AND DISCUSSION

(1) Make a list of all the different things enumerated as a failure or vanity. (2) Make a list of the different things coming to us as God's gift of providence. (3) Make a list of prudential maxims or rules which teach how to live rightly and to lift us above the tribulations and defeat of life. (4) Does the author think seeking pleasure the real business of life? (5) Does he deny the value of altruistic service? (6) Does he believe in the future life and in future rewards?

SONG OF SOLOMON

Name. The name of the book is *Song of Songs Which Is Solomon's.* It is also called Canticles, meaning Song of Songs, and is so-called perhaps, because of its very great beauty.

Subject. The subject is faithful love, seen in a woman who though subjected to the temptations of an oriental court, remains faithful to her old lover. She, a country girl of the north, attracts the attention of the king, who brings her to Jerusalem and offers her every inducement to become the wife of the king. But upon final refusal she is allowed to return home to her lover, a country shepherd lad.

Meaning of the Story. (1) To the Jews of that time it was a call to purity of life, for a return to those relations which God had ordained between man and woman. It was a protest against polygamy which had become almost universal. Indeed, they regarded it as setting forth the whole history of Israel. They had often gone away from God to whom they were plighted as this girl was tempted to turn from her lover. (2) To the Christian it sets forth in allegory Christ and His church as Bridegroom and Bride and the fullness of love which unites the believer and his Savior. The Christian must not yield to the temptations of the world and be untrue to Jesus. Thus the attitude of the girl illustrates the true Christian attitude. (3) To all the world there is shown the purity and constancy of a woman's love and devotion to her ideals. It furnishes an ideal which, if properly held up, would cast out of human society all those monstrous practices that come from unworthy ideals. It would purify the relation of the sexes and save us from the ruin of the social sin.

Style. It is part dialogue and part monologue. Their love on both sides is expressed in that sensual way common among the oriental peoples. Most of the allusions give rise to the belief that it was written to celebrate the nuptials of Solomon and the daughter of Pharaoh. It is a sort of drama, with three principal characters: Solomon, the Shulamite girl, and her shepherd lover.

ANALYSIS

I. The King's First Attempt to Win the Virgin's Love, 1:1-2:7.

1. She converses with the ladies of the court, 1:1-8.
2. The king's attempt fails to win her, 1:9-2:7.

II. The King's Second Effort to Win Her Love. 2:8-5:8.

1. The virgin recalls her former happiness when with her lover at home, 2:8-17.
2. In a dream she goes in search of him, 3:1-5.
3. The king shows her his glory and greatness, 3:6-11.
4. She again rejects his love in spite of his praises of her beauty, 4:1-7.
5. She longs for her absent lover, 4:8-5:1.
6. She dreams of seeking in vain for him, 5:2-8.

III. The King's Third Attempt to Win Her, 5:9-8:4.

1. The ladies of the court cannot understand her faithfulness to her old lover, 5:9-6:3.
2. The king's third effort to win her is met with the declaration of her purpose to remain true to her absent lover, 6:4-8:4.

IV. The Triumph of the Maiden, 8:5-14.

She returns to her home among the hills of the north and is reunited with her shepherd lover.

MESSAGES OF THE SONG OF SOLOMON

1. **On Human Love.** Love is the noblest expression of the human heart. Here are fundamental teachings about it. (1) Its basis. This is mutual satisfaction (2:2-3). The love of one supplements the love of the other and serves to exclude the love of anyone else. (2) Its strength. It is indestructible (8:6-7) and is an unquenchable fire. (3) Its blessing. It is a source of joy, rest, peace, and courage. (4) Its greatness. It is the greatest thing in human relationship and also the greatest thing in religion. It constitutes the highest ultimate value of life.

2. **On Religion.** Here are three suggestions: (1) Ours is primarily a religion of love. This will be most clear if we apply the basis, strength, etc., given above to this thought. (2) Human love is sanctified by religion which takes it out of the realm of lust. (3) Religious life finds its best interpretation in the terms of human love, such as fondness, self-abandonment, fidelity, etc.

FOR STUDY AND DISCUSSION

(1) Make a list of the passages by which the woman's beauty is described. (2) Passages that suggest the relation of the saved soul to Christ. (3) Passages that suggest the glory of the church. (4) Some of the passages by which the love of the woman and of the king is expressed. (5) The basis of human love, 2:2-3. (6) The strength of human love, 8:6-7. (7) The interpretation of human love in terms of divine love.

CHAPTER XIII

ISAIAH

Lesson 77. Introductory Discussions and Chs. 1-6.

Lesson 78. Isaiah, Chs. 40-48.

Lesson 79. Isaiah, Chs. 49-57.

Lesson 80. Isaiah, Chs. 58-66 and Messages of the book.

Prophet. In the study of the messages of the prophets we should understand that the meanings of the term prophet may be: (1) A person employed in the public utterance of religious discourse, very much as the preacher of today. This was the most common function of the prophet. Some were reformers while others were evangelists or revivalists. (2) One who performed the function of the scribes and wrote the history and biography and annals of their nations. In this capacity they compiled or wrote large portions of the books of the Old Testament. (3) One who was able to discern the future and foretell events which would transpire afterward. In this capacity he is called a seer and his predictions are of great concern. This kind of prophecy constitutes but a small portion of the prophetic books.

Early Prophets. The first great prophet was Moses who was followed during the period of the Judges by two, Deborah the prophetess (Judges 4:4) and an unnamed prophet (6:8). A little later there seemed to be many under the leadership of Samuel. Saul failed as king because he would not follow the leadership of the prophets. During succeeding years several appeared, but only occasionally. Among them are Nathan (II Sam. 12:1 ff.; I Kings 1:11) and Gad (II Sam. 24:11 ff). They even favored the division of the kingdom (I Kings 11:29 ff.; 12:22 ff.) thinking this was necessary to save true religion. The greatest of these earlier prophets were Elijah and Elisha who arose to combat idolatry that grew up especially under King Ahab who was influenced to it by Jezebel his heathen wife who worshipped Baal. They wrote no books, but finally drove out this evil worship from Israel.

The Prophetical Books. All take their name from the prophets whose messages they bear. They are written largely in the poetic style and are usually divided into two groups: (1) The major prophets which include Isaiah, Jeremiah, Lamentations, Ezekiel, and Daniel. (2) The minor prophets, including the other twelve. This division is based on the bulk of material in the books, and is unscientific and is also misleading, since it may suggest that some are more important than others. We are not capable of deciding the relative importance of their messages.

They are more appropriately divided according to their place in the prophetic order, or the period of Israel's history when they prophesied, somewhat as follows: (1) *The Pre-exilic prophets*, or those who prophesied before the exile. These are, (1) Jonah, Amos and Hosea, prophets of Israel; (2) Obadiah, Joel, Isaiah, Micah, Nahum, Habakkuk, Zephaniah, and Jeremiah, prophets of Judah. 2. *The exilic prophets*, Ezekiel and Daniel. Both are of Judah, but prophesy to the whole nation during the captivity. 3. *The Post-exilic prophets*, prophets who prophesied after the captivity. All are of Judah and are Haggai, Zechariah and Malachi.

Jeremiah's ministry perhaps extended into the period of the captivity. There is great uncertainty about the chronology of Obadiah, Joel, and Jonah. There is difference of opinion also as to whether certain of the prophets belong to Judah or to Israel. Micah is an example. The teacher should be able to give reasons for this difference.

The Study of the Prophets. The student should hold in mind that the prophet deals primarily with the moral and religious conditions of his own people at the time of his ministry. His denunciations, warnings, and exhortations are, therefore, not abstract principles, but are local and for Israel. The prophet was then first of all a Jewish patriot and revivalist filled with the Holy Ghost and with zeal for Israel.

The predictive elements of the prophetic books must be interpreted in the light: (1) Of a nearby or local fulfillment, such as of the dispersion and restoration. (2) Of a far off and greater fulfillment of which the first is only the forerunner, such as the advent of the Messiah and His glorious reign over the whole earth. *The interpretation of prophecy should generally be in the literal, natural and unforced meaning of the words.* The following passages will show how prophecy, already fulfilled, has been fulfilled literally, and not allegorically: Gen. 15:13-16; 16:11-12; Deut. 28:62-67; Ps. 22:1, 7, 8, 15-18; Isa. 7:14; 53:2-9; Hos. 3:4; Joel 2:28-29; Mic. 5:2; Acts 2:16-18; Matt. 21:4-5; Lu. 1:20, 31; Acts 1:5; Matt. 2:4-6; Lu. 21:16, 17, 24; Acts 21:10-11.

In a given book of prophecy, the book should be read carefully and all the different subjects which it treats noted. This should be followed by a careful study to find what is said about the several topics already found. To illustrate, the prophet may mention himself, Jerusalem, Israel, Judah, Babylon, or Egypt, etc. One should learn what is said of each. This will make necessary the student's learning all he can of the history of the different subjects mentioned that he may understand the prophecy about it.

The Prophet Isaiah. Several things are known of him. (1) He was called to his work the last year of the reign of Uzziah. (2) He lived at Jerusalem during the reigns of Uzziah, Jotham, Ahaz, and Hezekiah, and the most of his life seems to have been spent as a sort of court preacher or chaplain to the king. (3) He is the most renowned of all the Old Testament prophets, his visions not being restricted to his own country and times. He spoke for all nations and for all times. "He was a man of powerful intellect, great integrity, and remarkable force of character." (4) He is quoted more in the New Testament than any of the other prophets and, because of the relation of his teaching to New Testament times and teachings, his prophecies have been called the "bridge between the old and new covenants." (5) He married and had two sons.

Nature of His Teachings. In his inaugural vision, recorded in the sixth chapter, Isaiah has impressed upon him some truths that shaped his whole career. He saw: (1) The holiness and majesty of God. (2) The corruption of those about him. (3) The certainty of awful judgment upon the wicked. (4) The salvation of a remnant that was to be the seed of a new Israel. With these truths burning in his soul he pressed the battle of righteousness into every sphere of life. He strove to regenerate the entire national life. He tried to make not only religious worship, but commerce and politics so pure that it could all become a service acceptable to God. He, therefore, became a religious teacher, preacher, social reformer, statesman and seer. He felt that his nation had a divine mission and that God would care for it, but since it would not carry out His divine purpose, He would vindicate His divine justice by bringing judgment upon it. He, therefore, frequently predicted the doom of the nation.

Conditions of Israel (The Northern Kingdom). Isaiah began to prophesy when it was outwardly rich and prosperous under the rule of Jeroboam II. Inwardly it was very corrupt. It soon went to pieces, however (621 B. C.), being conquered and carried into captivity by the Assyrians.

Conditions of Judah (The Southern Kingdom). During the reigns of Ahaz, Jotham, and Uzziah, oppression, wickedness, and idolatry existed everywhere. Ahaz made an alliance with Assyria, which finally brought destruction to Israel, but Hezekiah listened to Isaiah and made reforms, and God destroyed the Assyrian army before Jerusalem was destroyed.

Nature of the Contents of the Book. The contents of the book of Isaiah have been said to include: (1) Warnings and threats against his own people because of their sins. (2) Sketches of the history of his times. (3) Prophecies of the return of Israel from captivity. (4) Prophecies concerning the coming of the Messiah. (5) Predictions of the judgment of God on other nations. (6) Discourses that urge upon Israel moral and religious reformation. (7) Visions of the future glory and prosperity of the church. (8) Expressions of thanksgiving and praise.

The Center of Interest. The prophet deals primarily with the nation and not with the individual. He speaks primarily of the present and not of the future. These two facts must be kept constantly in mind as we read and interpret the book.

ANALYSIS

NOTE. It is doubtful whether academy or high school students should even be required to learn any portion of the Analysis of this book. They should, however, read and discuss the portions assigned in the lesson scheme and might be assigned some topics, such as what is predicted against each of the foreign nations and a few passages that vividly describe the life and work of Jesus. The full Analysis, however, is given, and a large number of topics for study and discussion. This will serve the purpose of individuals and of classes that are more advanced.

I. Discourses Concerning Judah and Israel, Chs. 1-12.

1. Some promises and rebukes, Chs. 1-6.
   - (1) The great arraignment, Ch. 1.
   - (2) Zion's exaltation through the judgment of the sinful, Chs. 2-4.
   - (3) Lessons of the vineyard, Ch. 5.
   - (4) The prophet's call, Ch. 6.
2. The book of Immanuel, Chs. 7-12.
   - (1) Two interviews with Ahaz, Ch. 7.
   - (2) Some terrible judgments and a great deliverance, 8:1-9:7.
   - (3) God's punishment of wicked Samaria, 9:8-10:4.
   - (4) Destruction of Assyria and salvation of God's people, 10:5-12 end.

II. Prophecies Against Foreign Nations, Chs. 13-23.

In the order given there is a prophecy concerning the following nations, Babylon, Assyria, Philistia, Moab, Damascus with Israel and Judah, Ethiopia, Egypt, Assyria's overthrow of Ethiopia and Egypt, Second Message against Babylon, Dumah (Edom), Jerusalem and Tyre.

III. Judgment of the World and Triumph of God's people, Chs. 24-27.

1. Terrible judgments to come, Ch. 24.
2. Israel's triumph, Ch. 25.
3. Judah's song of praise, Ch. 26.
4. The oppressor judged for Israel's sake, Ch. 27.

IV. Judah's Relation to Egypt and Assyria, Chs. 28-32.

1. Fall of Samaria and punishment of sinful Judah, Ch. 28.
2. Siege and deliverance of Ariel (Jerusalem), Ch. 29.
3. Folly of relying on Egypt, Chs. 30-32.

V. Great Deliverance of Jerusalem, Chs. 33-39.

1. Woe to the cruel Assyrians and praise to the righteous, Ch. 33.
2. Overthrow of Edom and wonderful deliverance of God's people, Chs. 34-35.
3. Overthrow of Assyria, Chs. 36-37.
4. Hezekiah's recovery and embassy from Babylon, Chs. 38-39.

VI. God's Preparation for Certain Deliverance, Chs. 40-48.

1. God brings deliverance, Ch. 40.
2. Israel God's servant and the challenge to idols, Ch. 41.
3. Jehovah's servant and his work, Ch. 42.
4. God's grace will redeem Israel while idols can do nothing, 43:1-44:23.
5. The mission of Cyrus, 44:24-45 end.
6. Overthrow of Babylon and her gods, Chs. 46-47.
7. Exhortation and encouragement to be patient, Ch. 48.

VII. Deliverance Will Come Through Jehovah's Servant the Messiah, Chs. 49-57.

1. His servant will by divine strength deliver Zion, Chs. 49-50.
2. Trust God and expect deliverance and return to Jerusalem, 51:1-52:12.
3. Suffering, success and exaltation of Jehovah's servant, 52:13-53 end.

4. Happy prospect and invitation to prepare for the Lord's coming, Chs. 54-55.
5. Covenant blessing of the righteous and denunciations of wicked rulers and idolators in Israel, Chs. 56-57.

VIII. Restoration of Zion and Messianic Kingdom, Chs. 58-66.
1. Jehovah desires true not formal worship, Ch. 58.
2. Jehovah will redeem Zion after punishing her sins, Ch. 59.
3. Transcendent glory of Zion, Ch. 60.
4. Merciful program for the new age, Ch. 61.
5. A new picture of the glory of renewed Zion, Ch. 62.
6. Prayer of penitent Israel after God crushes Edom, their enemy, Chs. 63-64.
7. Jehovah answers the prayer and promises salvation to Judah, Chs. 65-66.

MESSAGES

No other book is richer in general lesson suggestions than this. Among those most noticeable to the average reader are:

1. Lessons Seen Everywhere on the Surface. (1) That God knows about man's calamity and sin. (2) That God is keenly interested in man and desires to help him. (3) That God sends messengers to tell man of his danger and of God's willingness to aid him.

2. Lessons on God's Government. There are four: (1) That government is for purposes of grace, while grace is for purposes of government. He governs us so that we may have grace and shows us grace that He may govern us. (2) That salvation by grace is followed by submission to control. (3) That God's principles of government are righteousness and justice. (4) That His government is characterized by patience, persistence, and power.

3. Lessons of Grace. We learn: (1) That sin violates grace. This is best seen later in the cross. (2) That human salvation depends upon submission to the activity of grace in the cross. (3) That human destiny is decided by response to the effect of the cross on man.

FOR STUDY AND DISCUSSION

(1) The sins of Israel and Judah that are rebuked. (2) Other nations against which he makes predictions and what he said of each. (3) Isaiah's call, Ch. 6. (4) Isaiah's errand to Ahaz, Ch. 7. (5) The way in which Isaiah rests the sole deity of Jehovah upon His ability to predict a future, Ch. 41. Give other illustrations. (6) The express predictions of the Messiah as we find them fulfilled in Jesus. (7) Point out the passages portraying the future glory of the church and the spiritual prosperity of the race. (8) Passages predicting the restoration of the Jews from captivity. (9) Some predictions already fulfilled: (a) God's judgments of the kings of Israel and the nation of Israel, Ch. 7. (b) The overthrow of Sennacherib, Ch. 37. (c) Disasters that were to overtake Babylon, Damascus, Egypt, Moab, and Idumea (Edom), Chs. 13, 15, 18, 19, and 34. (d) Vivid and marvelous descriptions of the final fate of Babylon and Idumea, 13:19-22; 34:10-17. (10) The theology of Isaiah or his views on such subjects as the moral condition of man, the need of a redeemer, the consequences of redemption, Divine Providence, the majesty and holiness of God, the future life, etc.

CHAPTER XIV

JEREMIAH AND LAMENTATIONS

Lesson 81. **Analysis, Introductory Discussions and Chapters 1, 37-45, and 52 of Jeremiah.**

Lesson 82. **Analysis, Introductory Discussions and Scripture of Lamentations and Messages of both books.**

JEREMIAH

Author. His name means *exalted of Jehovah,* and he is ranked second among the great Old Testament writers. He lived the last of the sixth and the first of the fifth centuries before Christ. His ministry began in 626 B. C., (the thirteenth year of Josiah (1:2), and lasted about sixty years, until after the fall of Jerusalem in 586 B. C. He probably died in Babylon during the early years of the captivity. He was of a sensitive nature, mild, timid, and inclined to melancholy. He was devoutly religious and naturally shrank from giving pain to others. He was uncommonly bold and courageous, although it was unpopular and subjected him to hatred and even to suffering wrong. He was unsparing in the denunciations and rebukes administered to his nation, not even sparing the prince. Everywhere there is a somber note of judgment and because of this he has been called a prophet of doom. He is also called the weeping prophet. He was distressed both by the disobedience and apostasy of Israel and by the evil which he foresaw. Being very devoutly religious, he was pained by the impiety of his time.

Condition of the Nations. (1) Israel, the northern kingdom, had been carried into captivity, and Judah stood alone against her enemies. (2) Judah had fallen into a bad state, but Josiah, who reigned when Jeremiah began his ministry, attempted to bring about reforms and restore the old order. After his death, however, wickedness grew more and more until, in the latter part of the life of Jeremiah, Jerusalem and the temple were destroyed by Nebuchadnezzar, and Judah was led away into captivity. (3) The world powers of the time of Jeremiah's birth were Assyria and Egypt. They were contending for supremacy. But Jerusalem lived to see both of them subdued and Babylon mistress of the world. He foresaw also how Babylon would fall and how a kingdom greater than all would rise wherein there would be righteousness and peace.

The Book. The book of Jeremiah is composed principally of sketches of biography, history, and prophecy, but the events and chapters are not in chronological order. It closes the period of the monarchy and marks the destruction of the holy city and of the sanctuary, and tells of the death agony of the nation of Israel, God's chosen people. But he saw far beyond the judgments of the near future to a brighter day when the eternal purpose of divine grace would be realized. The book, therefore, emphasizes the future glory of the kingdom of God, which must endure though Israel does perish. He saw this future glory: (1) As the salvation of a righteous remnant, 4:27; 5:10, 18; 30:11. (2) As the restoration of this remnant, 3:12, 21, 22; 16:14-15. (3) The rise of a new Jerusalem where God would dwell, 33:16. (4) As the coming of the Messianic king, 23:4-6; 30:9, 31. (5) As the new covenant of pardon and grace, 31:33, 34; 32:40; 33:8. (6) The presence of Jehovah among His people, 3:16. (7) As the turning of the nations to Jehovah, 3:17, 4:2; 16:19; 33:9. He made two special contributions to the truth as understood in his time. (1) The spirituality of religion. He saw the coming overthrow of their national and formal religion and realized that, to survive that crisis, religion must not be national, but individual and spiritual. (2) Personal responsibility (31:29-30). If religion was to be a spiritual condition of the individual, the doctrine of personal responsibility was a logical necessity. These two teachings constitute a great step forward.

I. **The Prophet's Call and Assurance,** Ch. 1.

II. **Judah Called to Repentance,** Chs. 2-22.
  1. Her sins set forth, Chs. 2-6.
  2. The call to repentance, Chs. 7-10.
  3. The appeal to the covenant, Chs. 11-13.
  4. Rejection and captivity foretold, Chs. 14-22.

III. **The Book of Consolation,** Chs. 23-33.
  1. The restoration of the remnant, Chs. 23-29.
  2. The complete restoration, Chs. 30-33.

IV. **The Doom of Jerusalem Due to the People's Wickedness,** Chs. 34-36.

V. **The History of Jeremiah and His Times,** Chs. 37-45.

VI. **Prophecies Against Foreign Nations,** Chs. 46-51.

VII. **Historical Appendix,** Ch. 52.

LAMENTATIONS

Name. The name means *elegies* or *mournful* or *plaintive poems.* It was formerly a part of Jeremiah and represents the sorrows of Jeremiah when the calamities which he had predicted befell his people, who had often despised and rejected him for his messages. He chose to live with them in their suffering, and out of his weeping pointed them to a star of hope. There are five independent poems in as many chapters. Chapters 1, 2, 4, and 5 have each 22 verses or just the number of letters of the Hebrew alphabet. Chapter 3 has 66 verses, or just three times the number of letters of the alphabet. The first four chapters mentioned (1, 2, 4, 5) are acrostic, that is, each verse begins with a letter of the Hebrew alphabet following the order of the alphabet. In chapter 3 each letter is used in order and is three times repeated as the initial letter of three successive lines. It is also of interest that in the chapters that have 66 verses each verse has only one third as many poetic measures as are found in the verses of the chapters that have only 22 verses, thus making the same number of measures, whether there are 22 or 66 verses. All of this shows how the poems were wrought with great care and diligence.

ANALYSIS

I. The Misery of Jerusalem, Ch. 1.

II. The Cause of the People's Suffering, Ch. 2.

III. The Basis of Hope, Ch. 3.

IV. The Past and Present of Israel, Ch. 4.

V. The Final Appeal for Restoration, Ch. 5.

MESSAGES

Lessons on Sin. Here are six teachings: (1) That sin will certainly be punished. (2) That sin grieves the heart of God. (3) That sin will be triumphed over by God. (4) That sin blinds men to their best interests. (5) That sin turns men against their best friends. (6) That sin destroys nations as well as individuals.

2. **Lessons on True Love.** (1) It does not blind us to the faults of those we love. Jeremiah saw Judah's sins. (2) It does not cover up faults, but tries to win us from them. Jeremiah sought to save Israel by telling of her sins. (3) It does not desert one who, heedless of warning, persists in sin and meets calamity. Jeremiah went with Judah into captivity and there wept over them.

FOR STUDY AND DISCUSSION

(1) Make a list of the evils predicted against the people because of their sins (Example: 19:7-9). (2) Make a list of the different sins and vices of which Jeremiah accuses Is-

rael (Example: 2:13; 3:20, etc.). (3) Point out all the prophecies of Divine judgment against other nations and analyze the punishment foretold (Example: 5:18-25). (4) Study the case of fidelity to parents given in Ch. 35. (5) Study all passages in both books which tell of the Messiah and of Messianic times and make a study of each (as 23:5-6). (6) Select a few of the striking passages of Lamentations and show how they apply to the facts of history. (7) The sign and type of the destruction of the land, Chs. 13-14. (8) The potter an illustration of God's power over nations, Chs. 18-19. (9) The illustration of the return, seen in the figs, Ch. 24. (10) Jeremiah's letter to the captive, Ch. 29. (11) Jeremiah's love for Judah—it saw their faults, rebuked them for their sins, but did not desert them when they were in suffering, because they despised his advice.

CHAPTER XV

EZEKIEL AND DANIEL

Lesson 82. Analysis, Introductory Discussion and Chapters 1-7 of Ezekiel.

Lesson 83. Ezekiel, Chs. 40-48 and Messages of the book.

Lesson 84. Analysis, Introductory Discussions and Chapters 1-6 of Daniel.

Lesson 85. Daniel, Chs. 7-12 and Messages of the book.

Lesson 86. Review of the studies in Chapters XIII to XV. In each of the five prophets studied review the topics "For Study and Discussion" on the portions of the books studied.

EZEKIEL

The Prophet. His name means *God will strengthen.* He was a priest and was carried into captivity by Nebuchadnezzar, B. C. 597. He had a home on the river Chebar where the Elders of Judah were accustomed to meet. His wife died in the ninth year of his captivity. He was a man of very powerful intellect and apparently from the better classes of those carried into captivity. He is less attractive than Isaiah and less constant in the flow of his thought than Jeremiah. He is not so timid or sensitive as Jeremiah, but has all the horror for sin and all of his grief occasioned by the wickedness of his people and the suffering which they endured. In his boldness of utterance he was not surpassed by any of his predecessors.

Nature of the Prophecy. The nature of the prophecy or the methods by which he exercised or manifested his prophetic gifts differs from that of the other prophets. He does not so much predict events as see visions of them. Allegories, parables, similitudes, and visions abound, some of them symbolic of the future and others of existing facts and conditions. The prophet remains on the banks of Chebar and in spirit is transported to Jerusalem and the temple. Much of the book is in character similar to Revelation, and while the general subjects are very plain, much of the meaning of the symbols is obscure. There are, however, powerful addresses and eloquent predictions of Divine judgments on the nations. It was probably due to the services of Ezekiel that Israel's religion was preserved during the exile.

His Teaching. He repeats all the great teachings of those who preceded him, laying special emphasis upon such matters as justice, morality, and spiritual religion, but manifesting less interest in ceremonialism (Chaps. 6-12; 7:22; 33:25). He joins Jeremiah in declaring the moral responsibility of the individual, and formulates in considerable detail the doctrines of repentance and forgiveness, particularly showing that repentance is necessary to salvation (Chaps. 14, 18, 33, especially 14:1-20; 18:20-32). He proclaims the necessity of a new heart and a new spirit (11:19; 18:31; 36:26). As a Messianic prophet he looked for the full and glorious restoration of the Jews under a theocracy with a complete national system centered in the temple, which has the services of both priests and Levites (11:16ff; 16:60ff; 17:22-24; 20:40ff; Chaps. 33:48). Both as priest and as prophet he desired to promote popular holiness and to correct some of the abuses that endangered the nation. In doing this he denounced Judah's sins and predicted the downfall of Jerusalem (Chaps. 1-24), and proclaimed coming judgments over foreign nations (Chaps. 25-32).

Condition of the Jews. (1) *Political and Social Condition.* They are captives living in Babylon, but are treated as colonists and not as slaves. They increased in numbers and accumulated great wealth and some of them rose to the highest offices. (2) *The religious condition or* *outlook.* They had religious freedom and in this period they forever gave up their idolatry. They sought out the books of the law, revised the canon, wrote some new books and perhaps inaugurated the synagogue worship which became so powerful afterward.

ANALYSIS

I. **Ezekiel's Call,** Chs. 1-3.

1. Preliminary vision, Ch. 1.
2. The call, Chs. 2-3.

II. **The Destruction of Jerusalem,** Chs. 4-24.

1. The siege and certain judgment of the city, Chs. 4-7.
2. The condition of the city and the sins of the people, Chs. 8-19.
3. Renewed proofs and predictions of the doom of Judah and Jerusalem, Chs. 20-24.

III. **Predictions Against Foreign Nations and Cities,** Chs. 25-32.

IV. **Prophecies Concerning the Restoration,** Chs. 33-48.

1. The restoration of Judah to the promised land, Chs. 33-39.
2. The Messianic times, Chs. 40-48.

MESSAGES OF EZEKIEL

(1) As to the terrible nature of sin. It tears down and destroys both men and nations. (2) As to individual responsibility. Men do not suffer for the sins of others, but for their own sins, 18:1-4; 33:10 ff. (3) As to the power and majesty of God. This is seen in the face of different animals such as the lion, ox, and eagle, and in His control of all circumstances. This power and majesty also becomes a basis of hope both that judgment will certainly come upon sin and that right will be victorious.

FOR STUDY AND DISCUSSION

(1) The condition, the particular sin and judgment promised upon each of the nations mentioned—has the prediction been fulfilled? (2) The duties and responsibilities of a

preacher as illustrated by Ezekiel's watchman, Chap. 33. (3) The vision of dry bones, Chap. 37. (4) Judah and Israel under the figure of an evil woman, Chap. 23. (5) The healing river, 47:1-12. (6) The teachings about the Restoration, in the following passage: 36:8; 9, 25-27, 29, 30, 34, 35; 37:1-14; 37:22, 26, 27; 43:11-12. (7) The symbols and types of the book.

DANIEL

Name. The name is taken from its leading character, Daniel, which means, *God is my Judge.* The author was probably Daniel himself, though some think it may have been one of his companions, and still others think the history may have been gotten together and written about 166 B. C.

The Date. The date then would have been between the captivity, 605 B. C., and the death of Daniel, 533 B. C., perhaps late in his life, or if by some other (which I do not think likely) about 166 B. C.

The Prophet. He was probably born in Jerusalem and was one of the noble young captives first carried into captivity by King Nebuchadnezzar, 605 B. C. He was educated by order of the king, and early distinguished himself by his stand against the luxury and idolatry of Babylonia. He soon rose to great favor and was chosen to stand before the king in one of the highest government positions under the Chaldean, Median, and Persian dynasties. He lived through the whole period of the captivity, and probably died in Babylon. It is said that not one imperfection of his life is recorded. The angel repeatedly calls him "greatly beloved." Four things of a miraculous nature are very important: (1) The interpretation of Nebuchadnezzar's dream which first brought him into prominence; (2) Overcoming the power of fire and escaping unhurt when cast into the fiery furnace; (3) His visions of Babylonia, Persia, Greece, and Rome, and of the eternal kingdom which God would set up; (4) His escaping alive when cast into the lion's den.

World Empires of the Book. (1) *The Babylonian Empire* (625-536 B. C.) with Nebuchadnezzar as the leading king and the one who carried Israel captive. (2) *The Persian Empire* (536-330 B. C.) which became a world power through Cyrus, under whom the Jews returned to Jerusalem. (3) *The Grecian Empire,* which, under the leadership of Alexander the Great, subdued the entire Persian World. (4) *The Roman Empire,* which was anticipated by, and grew out of, the Syrian Empire.

Purpose of the Book. The purpose of the book seems to be: (1) To magnify Jehovah, who delivers His servants, who is God of all nations, and who will punish idolatry, who is pure, righteous, etc. (2) To encourage his countrymen to resist the forces that threaten the foundation of their faith. This was done by the example of Daniel and his companions whom Jehovah saved. (3) To give a prophecy or vision of all times from the day of Daniel to the Messianic period. (4) To outline the religious philosophy of history which would issue in a great world state, which the Messianic King would rule by principles of justice and right, and which would subdue all kingdoms and have everlasting dominion. The main idea is the ultimate triumph of the kingdom of God. As compared with former prophetic books, there are two new teachings: (1) Concerning angels. (2) Concerning a resurrection from the dead.

ANALYSIS

I. Daniel's History, Chs. 1-6.
   1. His youth and education, Ch. 1.
   2. Interpretation of Nebuchadnezzar's image dream, Ch. 2.
   3. In the fiery furnace, Ch. 3.
   4. Interpretation of Nebuchadnezar's tree dream, Ch. 4.
   5. Interpretation of the hand-writing on the wall for Belshazzar, Ch. 5.
   6. In the lions' den, Ch. 6.

II. Daniel's Vision of the Kingdom, Chs. 7-12.

1. The four beasts, Ch. 7.
2. The ram and the he-goat, Ch. 8
3. The seventy weeks, Ch. 9.
4. The final vision, Chs. 10-12.

MESSAGES OF DANIEL

(1) Concerning God's wisdom and power. He reveals His wisdom through His people whom He knows and who know Him. His power is magnified in the care of His people for whose good He overrules all things. (2) Concerning human governments. God sets up and destroys nations. He allows the evil nation to develop and then destroys it and develops the good and preserves it. In this way He governs all the world toward purposes of grace, and shows that He has power and wisdom to govern it to the end of time. (3) Concerning the growth and conflict of good and evil. Evil grows more and more determined, while good grows more and more distinct. Hence the question, "Is the world getting better?" and the result that evil and good must ultimately meet in conflict. (4) Concerning right living. One can do right in spite of surroundings (see Daniel). It may cost heavy trials of faith, but will make men know the power of God. (5) Concerning the Messianic kingdom. It will be a great world power, ruled by justice and right. It will destroy all other kingdoms and will last forever.

FOR STUDY AND DISCUSSION

(1) Make a list of the various visions of Daniel and become familiar with the contents of each. (2) Make a list of all the passages that refer to the fact of Daniel's praying and point out some of the specific prayers with their answers. (3) Point out the different attempts to overthrow or kill Daniel and tell the cause, by whom he was opposed and how he escaped. (4) Make a list of the different symbols such as the lion and learn the description given of each

symbolic animal. (5) Point out the several decrees made by the different kings and learn what led to the decree, how it affected Daniel, how it bore upon the worship of the people of his nation, how it affected the worship of Jehovah, etc. (6) The difficulty and possibility of right living in bad surroundings. (7) The openness of Daniel's conduct. (8) The elements of strength of character displayed by Daniel. (9) The inevitable conflict between good and evil.

CHAPTER XVI

HOSEA, JOEL AND AMOS

Lesson 87. Analysis, Introductory Discussions and Chs. 1-8 of Hosea.

Lesson 88. Hosea, Chs. 9-14. Messages of the book and topics "For Study and Discussion."

Lesson 89. Book of Joel, including Analysis, Discussions of the book, Messages, topics "For Study and Discussion" and Scripture reading.

Lesson 90. Discussion of the book of Amos and Amos, Chs. 1-6.

Lesson 91. Amos, Chs. 7-8, Messages and Analysis of the book and topics "For Study and Discussion."

HOSEA

The Prophet. He is called the *Prophet of Divine Love.* His name, Hosea, means *Deliverance.* He was a native and citizen of Israel and followed Amos whom he may have heard in Bethel. He was a contemporary of Isaiah, and bore faithful testimony to corrupt Israel in the North, while Isaiah prophesied at Jerusalem, and was to Israel what Jeremiah became to Judah. He was prepared for his work through the lessons which he learned from the sins of his unfaithful wife. (1) Through the suffering which he endured because of her sons, he understood how God was grieved at the wickedness of Israel and how her sins were not only against God's law, but an insult to divine love. (2) In love and at great cost he restored his wayward wife, and in that act saw a hope of the restoration and forgiveness of Israel. His ministry extended over more than sixty years and was perhaps the longest of any on record. It continued 786-726 B. C., covering the last few years of the reign of Jeroboam II, to which Chs. 1-3 belong, and the period of anarchy following.

Style and Method. His style, is "abrupt, uneven, inelegant," but also poetical, figurative, and abounding in metaphors. His writings must be interpreted with great care to get what is meant by his symbolic speech. He reminds one of modern reformers and revivalists. Through all the anger which the book reveals we see also the surpassing beauty of reconciling love. One sees everywhere that the supreme goal to which Hosea moves is the re-establishment of Israel's fellowship of life and love with Jehovah.

Conditions of Israel. *Outwardly* there was prosperity. Syria and Moab had been conquered; commerce had greatly increased; the borders of the land had been extended and the temple offerings were ample. *Inwardly* there was decay. Gross immoralities were being introduced; worship was being polluted and the masses of the people crushed, while the Assyrian Empire was advancing and ready to crush Israel, whom, because of her sins, God had abandoned to her fate.

They countenanced oppression, murder, lying, stealing, swearing, etc. They had forgotten the law and their covenant to keep it, and had substituted the worship of Baal for that of Jehovah, thereby, becoming idolators. They no longer looked to God in their distress, but turned to Egypt and Assyria for help, and thereby put security and prosperity on a basis of human strength and wisdom instead of resting them upon a hope of divine favor.

ANALYSIS

I. Israel's Sin, illustrated by the tragedy of Hosea's unfortunate marriage, Chs. 1-3.

1. **His evil wife and their children, Ch. 1.**
2. **Israel's unfaithfulness and return to God seen in the evil woman, Ch. 2.**
3. **God's love restores Israel as Hosea does his wife. Ch. 3.**

II. The Prophetic Discourses, Chs. 4-14.

1. Israel's sin, Chs. 4-8.
2. Israel's coming punishment, Chs. 9-11.
3. Israel's repentance and restoration, Chs. 12-14.

MESSAGES OF HOSEA

1. On National Decay. These lessons may be applied to our day. (1) There was political apostasy. They quit seeking God and sought the help of Egypt and Assyria, 7:11. (2) There was religious aspostasy. The worship of Baal was substituted for that of Jehovah, 8:5-7. (3) There was moral apostasy, which was manifested by lying, stealing, etc., 4:2. (4) There was covenant apostasy. They forgot the law which they covenanted to keep, 4:6.

2. On the Nature and Effect of Sin. (1) Its nature. It is infidelity to love. God acted in love to them, they received His gifts of love and then played traitor to them. It is spiritual adultery—playing the harlot with the world. (2) Its effect. It silences testimony for God, profanes the name of God and brings punishment to them. Judgment is then the necessary result of sin and cannot be averted, if the sin is persisted in.

3. On Love. It is unconquerable, but suffers when sinned against. Through its self-forgetfulness it triumphs over the sinner and pardons him when he submits.

FOR STUDY AND DISCUSSION

(1) Make a list of all the exhortations to repentance and reformation and study them. (2) Point out the different utterances of judgment upon the people. (3) Make a list of the expressions of tender love for the wayward and backsliding one. (4) Make a list of all passages indicating grief and suffering because of the sin and danger of the one loved. (5) Political and religious apostasy. (6) Sin as infidelity to love—as spiritual adultery. (7) The invitations of the book.

JOEL

The Prophet. His name means *Jehovah is God,* but his birthplace and conditions of life are unknown. He very probably prophesied in Judah (2:15-17), and the time of his ministry is commonly thought to have been during the reign of Joash, king of Israel, and Amaziah, king of Judah. It seems certain that his is one of the earliest (some think the very earliest) of the prophetic books, and his references to the temple and its services have caused some to conclude that he was a priest.

The Prophecy. (1) The occasion of the prophecy was four successive plagues of insects, particularly the locusts (2:25), and a drouth (2:23), which had been unprecedented. These calamities, declares the prophet, are the result of their sins and should call them to repentance, that God may bless instead of curse their land. (2) The people repent and the calamity is removed. This is used by the prophet to foreshadow the coming destruction and restoration of Israel, and this restoration is also doubtless used to prefigure the Christian Church and its triumph on earth. (3) The great subject is the terrible judgments of God which were to come upon the people because of their sins. (4) His great distinctive prophecy is 2:28-32, which was fulfilled on the day of Pentecost, Acts 2:16-21. (5) In it all, he is emphasizing the rewards of the righteous and certain punishment of the wicked, and thus he appealed to both the hopes and the fears of men. But the chief value of the book is its optimism. There was victory ahead, the righteous would finally triumph and be saved, and God's enemies destroyed. The conflict of good and evil and of Israel and her enemies will end in entire and glorious triumph for Israel and right.

ANALYSIS

I. The Call to Repentance, Chs. 1:1-2:17.

1. **By the past scourge of locusts and drought, Ch. 1.**
2. **By the scourge to come, 2:1-17.**

II. Israel's Repentance and Jehovah's Promised Blessing, 2:18-3:21.

1. Material blessing, 2:18-27.
2. In the world judgment, Ch. 3.

MESSAGES OF JOEL

(1) Some principles of God's government. He governs in patience, by using the forces of nature and in grace that we may be blessed. (2) As to our place in His government. We are to recognize our place and then "to proclaim the fulness of the spirit" and "to urge men to call upon the Lord."

FOR STUDY AND DISCUSSION

(1) Point out the different statements about the drouth and locusts that indicate their severity and ruinous effects. (2) Collect the passages referring to the Messianic age and try to see how or what each foretells of that age. (3) Point out all references to the sins of Israel. (4) Collect evidences of the divine control of the universe as seen in the book.

AMOS

The Prophet. His name means *Burden,* and he is called prophet of righteousness. His home was at Tekoa, a small town of Judea about twelve miles south of Jerusalem, where he acted as herdsman and as dresser of sycamore trees. He was very humble, not being of the prophetic line, nor educated in the schools of the prophets for the prophetic office. God called him to go out from Judah, his native country, as a prophet to Israel, the Northern Kingdom. In obedience to this call he went to Bethel, where the sanctuary was, and delivered his bold prophecy. His bold preaching against the land of Israel while at Bethel aroused Amaziah, the leading idolatrous priest, who complained of him to the king. He was expelled from the kingdom, after he had denounced Amaziah, who had perhaps accused him of preaching as a trade, 7:10-14, but we know nothing more of him except what is in this book, which he perhaps wrote after he returned to Tekoa.

Time of the Prophecy. It was during the reign of Uzziah, king of Judah, and of Jeroboam II, king of Israel, and was outwardly a very prosperous time in Northern Israel. But social evils were everywhere manifest, especially the sins that grow out of a separation between the rich and poor, 2:6-8, etc. Religion was of a low and formal kind, very much of the heathen worship having been adopted.

Significance of the Prophecy. One need but read the book of Amos to see that he expects doom to come upon foreign nations, that he foretells the wickedness of the Jews and their coming doom, showing how the nation is to be dissolved and sold into captivity and that he predicts the glory and greatness of the Messianic kingdom. He thinks of Jehovah as the one true God, an all-wise, all-powerful, omnipresent, merciful, and righteous Person whose favor can only be secured by a life of righteousness. He sees that justice between men is the foundation of society, but men are responsible for their acts, that punishment will follow failure to measure up to our responsibility, that worship is an insult to God, unless the worshiper tries to conform to divine demands.

ANALYSIS

I. **The Condemnation of the Nations,** Chs. 1-2.

1. Introduction, 1:1-2.
2. Israel's neighbors shall be punished for their sins, 1:3-2:5.
3. Israel's sin shall be punished, 2:6-16.

II. **The Condemnation of Israel,** Chs. 3-6.

1. For evil iniquities, Ch. 3.
2. For oppression of the poor and for idolatry, Ch. 4.
3. Repeated announcements of judgment with appeals to return and do good, Chs. 5-6.

III. Five Visions Concerning Israel, Chs. 7:1-9:10.

1. The locusts, 7:1-3.
2. The fire, 7:4-6.
3. The plumb line (a testing), 7:7-9, a historical interlude (the conflict with Amaziah, 7:10-17).
4. A basket of summer fruit (iniquity ripe for punishment), Ch. 8.
5. The destruction of the altar (no more services), 9:1-10.

IV. Promised Restoration and Messianic Kingdom, 9:11-15.

MESSAGES OF AMOS

(1) Jehovah is not only the God of Israel and Judah, but of all nations. (2) He directs and governs all on the same principles of truth. (3) He knows international relationships and the obligations growing out of them. (4) The more enlightened nations have the greater responsibility. (5) National sins may for a time go unpunished, but repentance is the only way of final escape from doom on account of them. (6) The chosen people must be righteous or suffer.

FOR STUDY AND DISCUSSION

(1) Gather from the book a list of illustrations, sayings, etc., that are taken from the rustic or agricultural usages. (2) Make a list of the different nations against which he prophesies and point out the sin of each and the nature of the punishment threatened. (3) Make a list of the different illustrations used to show the greatness and power of God. (4) The sin of wrong inter-relation of nations. (5) The responsibility of national enlightenment. (6) Repentance as seen in this book. (1) The book's evidence of the luxury of the time.

CHAPTER XVII

OBADIAH, JONAH, AND MICAH

Lesson 92. The books of Obadiah and Jonah—Scripture reading, Analysis, Introductory, Discussions and topics "For Study and Discussion."

Lesson 93. The book of Micah, including Analysis, Introductory Discussions, Messages, reading of the Scripture and topics "For Study and Discussion."

OBADIAH

The Prophet.. His name means *Servant of the Lord*, but we know nothing of him except what we can gather from his prophecy. It was doubtless written after the fall of Jerusalem under Nebuchadnezzar, 587 B. C., and before the destruction of Edom, five years later, which would make the date about 585 B. C. This would make him a contemporary of Jeremiah.

Occasion. The occasion of the prophecy is the cruelty of the Edomites in rejoicing over the fall of Jerusalem and Judah. Judah had suffered and Edom was glad of it. It teaches that God's displeasure and judgment rest upon those who rejoice in the calamity of others, and especially upon those who rejoice or glory in the misfortunes of God's people. It further teaches that Jehovah is especially interested in His people and that He will establish a new kingdom with Judah and Jerusalem as the center, and with holiness as its chief characteristic.

The Jews. It is said to be a favorite book with the Jews because of the vengeance which it pronounces upon Edom, their brother. Its chief importance lies in its predictions of doom upon Edom, the descendants of Esau, the "twin brother of Jacob, who from the beginning had been hostile to Israel and became a type of the unchangeable hostility of the flesh to that which is born of the spirit."

ANALYSIS

I. Edom's Punishment, 1-9.

1. **She must fall, 1-4.**
2. **Her allies will desert her, 5-7.**
3. **Her wisdom will fail her, 8-9.**

II. Edom's Sin, 10-14.

III. Guilt of the Nations, 15-16.

IV. Judah Shall Be Restored, 17-21.

MESSAGES OF OBADIAH

(1) Lesson on sin. Concerning sin Obadiah suggests: (a) That its chief element is pride. This is manifested on the one hand in an animal-like baseness and godlessness, and displays a lack of spiritual sense; on the other, a defiance to God which looks to self-protection and asks, "Who shall bring me down?" (b) That its chief manifestation is violence, and is seen in the Edomites' opposition to Jacob and in their glorifying in and helping to crush Judah. (c) That its final issue is retribution. We shall reap what we sow—"As thou hast done, it shall be done to thee." (2) Lesson of hope for Israel. Edom (Esau) shall be destroyed, but Jacob shall be restored and perfected.

FOR STUDY AND DISCUSSION

(1) The sin of pride. (2) The sin of rejoicing in another's misfortune. (3) Punishment according to our sin and of the same kind as was our sin.

JONAH

The Prophet. His name means *dove*, and he is the son of Amittai. His home was Gath-heper, a village of Zebulun, and he, therefore, belonged to the ten tribes and not to Judah. He is first mentioned in II Kings 14:25, where he prophesied the success of Jeroboam II in his war with Syria, by which he would restore the territory that other nations had wrested from Israel. He likely prophesied at an early date, though all attempts to determine the time of his prophecy or the time and place of his death have failed.

The Prophecy. It differs from all other prophecies in that it is a narrative and more "the history of a prophecy than prophecy itself." All the others are taken up chiefly with prophetic utterances, while this book records the experiences and work of Jonah, but tells us little of his utterances. The story of Jonah has been compared to the stories of Elijah and Elisha (I Kings 17-19, and II Kings 4-6).

Although full of the miraculous element, the evident purpose is not to tell us about the prophet Jonah, but to teach great moral and spiritual lessons, and it is unfortunate that its supernatural element has made this book the subject of infidel attack. But the facts, though extraordinary, are in no way contradictory or inconsistent. Indeed, Mr. Driver has well said that "no doubt the outlines of the narrative are historical." Christ spoke of Jonah and accredited it by likening His own death for three days to Jonah's three days in the fish's belly. We shall emphasize its great moral and spiritual truths rather than its miraculous element.

It is the most "Christian" of all the Old Testament books, its central truth being the universality of the divine plan of redemption. Nowhere else in the Old Testament is such stress laid upon the love of God as embracing in its scope the whole human race. It aims to show the Jews that in their selfishness they had forgotten that He was anxious for all men to repent so that He could save them. It is a call to world-wide missions, and shows that those who know the Savior and His divine love are obligated to bear the message to all others.

ANALYSIS

I. Jonah's First Call and Flight from Duty, Chs. 1-2.
1. **The call, flight and punishment, 1:1-16.**
2. **The repentance and rescue, 1:17-2:10 end.**

II. Jonah's Second Call and Preaching at Nineveh, Ch. 3.
1. **His second call, verses 1-2.**
2. **His preaching against Nineveh, 3-4.**
3. **Nineveh repents, 5-9.**
4. **Nineveh is spared, 10.**

III. Jonah's Anger and God's Mercy, Ch. 4.
1. **Jonah's anger, verses 1-4.**
2. **The lesson of the gourd, 5-11.**

MESSAGES OF JONAH

1. **On God's Love and Care for Heathen Nations.** This is seen in the dealings of God with Nineveh. His attitude toward it was one of pity (4:11) and His efforts for it were earnest. He sent them a message and removed the judgment when they repented. All this sets forth God's love for the sinful city and is especially a foreign mission enterprise.

2. **On God and His Servants.** God needs and sends messengers. He patiently persists in His claims on them until they go. We cannot escape Him.

3. **On Our Failure in Duty.** We commonly fail because we are ignorant of God or misunderstand Him, and because we don't love the foreigners (as Jonah hated Nineveh). We can overcome by obedience to God, which will result in love to men.

4. **On True Repentance and God's Forgiveness.** Jonah, the sailors, and the city of Nineveh are all examples of how

nothing but genuine fear and repentance can bring deliverance from Jehovah. They also show that whoever does really repent will be forgiven.

5. **On the Function of the Preacher or Prophet.** It is his duty to preach just the message God gives him, to preach it where God tells him, to be fearless of death and unconcerned for personal interests, and not to worry about results—leave that to God.

6. **On the Jew's Claim that God Cares for Him Only.** This is shown to be false by God's desire to send a prophet to Nineveh, by His punishment of Jonah for his unwillingness to go, and by His forgiveness of Nineveh when she repented.

FOR STUDY AND DISCUSSION

(1) The different elements of character noticeable in Jonah. (2) The dangers of disobedience, to self and to others. (3) The possibilities of influence for the man commissioned of God. Jonah's influence on the sailors and on Nineveh. (4) God's care for heathen nations (4:11), and its bearing upon the Foreign Mission enterprise. (5) The nature of true repentance and God's forgiveness. (6) The prophet or preacher—his call, his message, and place of service.

MICAH

The Prophet. His name means *Who is the Lord?* and he was a native of Moresheth, a small town of Gath. He was a younger contemporary of Isaiah and prophesied to both Israel and Judah during the time of Jotham, Ahaz, and Hezekiah, kings of Judah; and of Pekah and Hosea, the last two kings of Israel. He sympathized deeply with the common people, being moved by the social wrongs of his time (Chs. 2-3), and became the people's advocate and defender as well as their accuser. He added no essentially new teaching to those of his predecessors but sought in a simple and forceful way to impress upon the people the fundamental truths of the religion of Jehovah. He clearly set forth the wickedness of Judah and Israel, their punishment, their restoration and the coming of Christ, and was partly responsible for the reformation under Hezekiah. As compared with Isaiah, he was a simple countryman, born of obscure parentage and recognized as one of the peasant class, while Isaiah was a city prophet of high social standing and a counselor of kings. Both alike, however, had firm convictions concerning the nature and the ultimate triumph of the Kingdom of God. Both had high conceptions of the character of Jehovah and of the obligations resting on His people.

Great Truths of the Prophecy are: (1) The destruction of Israel (1:6-7). (2) The desolation of Jerusalem and the temple (3:12 and 7:13). (3) The carrying off of the Jews to Babylon (4:10). (4) The return from captivity with peace and prosperity, and with spiritual blessing (4:1-8 and 7:11-17). (5) The ruler of Zion (Messiah) (4:8). (6) Where and when He should be born (5:2). This is his great prophecy and is accepted as final in the announcement to Herod.

ANALYSIS

I. The Impending Calamity, Ch. 1.

II. The Sins That Have Brought on This Calamity, Chs. 2-3.

1. In their wickedness they refuse to hear the prophets and are led into captivity, 2:1-11.
2. The promised restoration, 2:12-13.
3. The sins of the rich and of those in authority, Ch. 3.

III. The Promised Restoration and Glory, Chs. 4-5.

1. The promised restoration of the city of Zion, 4:1-5.
2. The restoration and glory of Israel, 4:6-13.
3. The mighty Messianic king to be given, Ch. 5.

IV. God's Controversy with Israel, Chs. 6-7.

1. God's charge and threat against them, Ch. 6.
2. In lamentation and patience the righteous must wait for a better time, 7:1-13.
3. God will have mercy and restore, 7:14-20.

MESSAGES OF MICAH

1. **On False Authority.** This is found in relation to three classes. (1) Civil rulers who judge for reward, are evil-hearted, love evil and hate good. (2) Spiritual rulers who teach for pay, claim to lean on God and are corrupted by bad motives. (3) Moral rulers who "divine for money," whose influence makes the people err and who make war while they cry peace.

2. **On True Authority.** Its coming is from the everlasting past. Its administration shall continue forever and shall feed (satisfy) God's people. Its final issue will result in the destruction of false methods and will bring peace.

FOR STUDY AND DISCUSSION

(1) The several accusations and threatenings against Israel and Judah. (2) The different things mentioned to describe the coming prosperity of Israel and of the Messianic period. (3) The false authority of civil rulers, or moral leaders, or spiritual teachers.

CHAPTER XVIII

NAHUM, HABAKKUK, ZEPHANIAH AND HAGGAI

Lesson 94. **The books of Nahum and Habakkuk, Analysis, Introductory Discussions, Messages, topics, "For Study and Discussion" and Scripture reading for both books.**

Lesson 95. **The books of Zephaniah and Haggai. Analysis, Introductory Discussions, Messages, topics "For Study and Discussion" and Scripture reading for both books.**

NAHUM

The Prophet. His name means *Consolation,* which seems to be in harmony with his mission, and he was a native of Elkosh, a small town of Galilee. We do not know where he uttered his prophecy, whether from Philistia, or Nineveh. It is thought that he escaped into Judah when the Captivity of the Ten Tribes began, and that he was at Jerusalem at the time of the Assyrian invasion. If the above conclusions are to be relied upon, the date of the prophecy would be in the reign of Hezekiah, king of Judah, which would be between 720 and 698 B. C. Others put it between the destruction of Thebes, 664 B. C. and the fall of Nineveh, 607 B. C., claiming that it might be either during the reign of Josiah, 640-625 B. C., or in the reign of Manasseh, 660 B. C.

The theme of the book is the approaching fall of Nineveh, the capital of Assyria, which held sway for centuries, and has been regarded as the most brutal of the ancient heathen nations. The purpose, in keeping with the name of the author, was to comfort his people, so long harassed by Assyria, which was soon to fall and trouble them no more. The style is bold and fervid and eloquent, and differs from all the prophetic books so far studied in that it is silent concerning the sins of Judah. It is a sort of outburst of exultation over the distress of a cruel foe, a shout of triumph over the downfall of an enemy that has prevented the exultation of the people of Jehovah. He emphasizes vengeance and mercy as the twofold manifestation of divine holiness, one resulting in the destruction of the wicked (1:2), the other in the salvation of the righteous (1:15; 2:2). He also reminds us of God's absolute sovereignty over the world and of His demand for personal and national righteousness in us.

ANALYSIS

I. The Doom of Nineveh Pronounced, Ch. 1.
II. The Siege and Fall of Nineveh, Ch. 2.
III. The Sins Which Will Cause Nineveh's Ruin, Ch. 3.

MESSAGES OF NAHUM

(1) Concerning man's sins which are punished. As indicated here, they are pride, which is a sin toward God; cruelty, which is a sin directed toward man; impenitence, which is determined resistance and must be punished. (2) Concerning God's love. This is shown in the avenging of His people and teaches us that His love is the condition of safety to a trusting soul. His wrath can never be understood except in the light of His love.

FOR STUDY AND DISCUSSION

(1) The striking features of the divine character seen in the book. How many in 1:2-3? (2) The description of Nineveh—not only her wickedness, but her energy and enterprise. (3) The doom predicted for Nineveh—analyze the predictions, showing the different things to which she is doomed. (4) Pride as a Godward sin and its punishment. (5) Cruelty, the manward sin and its punishment.

HABAKKUK

The Phophet. His name means *Embracing,* and he very likely was a contemporary of Jeremiah and prophesied between 608 B. C. and 628 B. C., and hence at a time of political and moral crisis. He may have been a Levite connected with the temple music.

The Prophecy. As Nahum prophesied the fall of Assyria for its oppression of Israel, Habakkuk tells of God's judgments upon the Chaldeans because of their oppression. The style is poetical and displays a very fine imagery. (1) There is a dialogue between the prophet and the Divine Ruler. (2) There is a prayer or psalm which is said not to be excelled in any language in the grandeur of its poetical conceptions and sublimity of expression.

Its purpose grew out of the fact that they were no better off under the rule of Babylon (Chaldeans) which had overthrown Assyria than they were formerly while Assyria ruled over them. He does not teach as other prophets do, but addresses God and questions the justice if not the reality of divine providence. It intended to answer the questions: (1) How could God use such a wicked instrument as the Chaldeans (Barbarians) to execute His purposes. (2) Could the Divine purpose be justified in such events? God's righteousness needed vindicating to the people. But he questions if it can be vindicated so long as the righteous suffer and the wicked triumph. (3) Why does wickedness seem to triumph while the righteous suffer? This is the question of Job, applied to the nation.

ANALYSIS

I. The Problem of the Apparent Triumph of Sin, Ch. 1.

1. **Why does sin go unpunished? Verses 1-4.**
2. **God says He has used the Chaldeans to punish sin, 5-11.**
3. **Are they to continue as evil forever? 12-17.**

II. The Impending Punishment of the Chaldeans, Ch. 2.

1. Waiting for the vision, verses 1-3.
2. Vision of five destructive woes, 4-20.

III. An Age of Confidence in God, Ch. 3.

1. Prayer of the disquieted prophet, verses 1-2.
2. Past history has shown that God will finally destroy Israel's enemies, 3-15.
3. The prophet must joyously trust God and wait when in perplexity, 16-19.

MESSAGES OF HABAKKUK

Three lessons are of importance. (1) That God will do right in the government of nations. (2) That sinful nations will finally perish. The Chaldeans will sin and die. (3) That the righteous shall prevail (live) by faith. We are encouraged to trust God and wait.

FOR STUDY AND DISCUSSION

(1) The morals of the people. (2) The character and deeds of the Chaldeans. (3) The universal supremacy of Jehovah. (4) The proper attitude amid perplexing problems. (5) Faith and faithfulness as a guarantee of supremacy and life.

ZEPHANIAH

The Prophet. He is a son of Cushi, a descendant of Hezekiah, and prophesied about 630 B. C. during the reign of Josiah. His prophecies may have aided in inaugurating and in carrying to success the reforms of Josiah. His name means *Hid of the Lord,* and he is supposed to have been a contemporary of Habakkuk.

The Prophecy. The prophecy seems to be based upon the ravages of the Scythians, whom the prophet considered the executioners of a divine judgment upon his sinful countrymen and surrounding nations, whom the nations had come to fear and whom Egypt had bribed. It looks to the judgment of the Lord which cannot be escaped except through repentance. He sees destruction of the unrepentant and exaltation and glory for the repentant. Its theme, therefore, is, "The great day of the Lord," in which suffering will come upon all nations with which the prophet is familiar, Jerusalem and all Judea included. Converts would be won from all parts of the world, and these could worship Jehovah, "every one from his place."

ANALYSIS

I. **The Coming Day of Wrath, Ch. 1.**
   1. The destruction of all things, verses 1-6.
   2. The severe punishment of Judah, 7-18.

II. **Judgment Upon Evil Nations, 2:1-3:7.**
   1. A plea for repentance, 2:1-3.
   2. The doom that shall engulf the nations, 2:4 end.
   3. Judah's obstinacy in sin, 3:1-7.

III. **Promised Blessing of the Faithful Remnant, 3:8-20.**
   1. Because of Israel's sin, the nation will be cleansed by punishment and converted to God, 3:8-10.
   2. Purified Israel shall be honored in all the earth, 3:11-20.

MESSAGES OF ZEPHANIAH

(1) That all nations as well as Judah must account for sin, Ch. 2. (2) That God's judgments aim both to punish sin and to purge and remedy the nation. (3) That in the past prophecy has been fulfilled as in the case of the destruction of Egypt and Assyria. (4) That all nations shall be converted, and instead of all nations coming to Jerusalem, men will worship God everywhere, 2:11, etc. (5) That there is to be a day of the restoration of the Lord. This will be a direct supernatural act of God and will affect man and all he has polluted. It will displace the bad with good, service will replace selfishness, etc.

FOR STUDY AND DISCUSSION

(1) Gather a list of all that is said to induce repentance or the turning away from evil. (2) What sins are condemned in Judah and other nations? Make a list of them. (3) Name the special classes that are condemned, as princes. (4) Make a list of the blessings promised for the coming Messianic days. (5) The purpose of the Lord's judgments.

HAGGAI

The Prophet. Haggai was born in Babylon and was one of those who returned from captivity under Zerubbabel, according to the decree of Cyrus. He prophesied during the period of the rebuilding of the temple, as recorded in Ezra, and was the first prophet called to prophesy after the Jews returned from the captivity in Babylon. He began his teaching sixteen years after the return of the first band to Jerusalem.

Conditions out of Which Grew the Prophecy. Under the decree of Cyrus, king of Persia, Zerubbabel, a descendant of King David, had led a company of captives back to Jerusalem. They had set up the altar and work on the temple had been begun, but the work had been interrupted by the hostile Samaritans and others, and for about fourteen years nothing had been done. These years of inactivity had dulled their zeal, and they were rapidly becoming reconciled to the situation, and by reason of their weakness, compared with the great task before them, they were beginning to despair of seeing their people and beloved city and temple restored to that glory pictured by former prophets.

The Prophecy. Its purpose was to restore the hope of the people and to give them zeal for the cause of God. This was accomplished by means of four distinct visions, each of which shows their folly in not completing the work, and promises divine blessing. He recognizes the importance of the temple as a religious center, and directed all of his utterances toward the subject of the rebuilding of the house of God. They hear God say, "I am with you, and will bless you." The result is seen in that they are enabled, in spite of opposition, to finish and dedicate it in about four years.

ANALYSIS

I. **The Appeal to Rebuild the Temple,** Ch. 1.
   1. **The appeal, verses 1-11.**
   2. **The preparations to build, 12-15.**

II. **The New Temple, 2:1-19.**
   1. **The superior glories of it, 2:1-9.**
   2. **The blessing of its holy service, 2:10-19.**

III. **The Messianic Kingdom, 2:20-23.**

MESSAGES OF HAGGAI

(1) That false content and discontent are dangerous. (2) That false fears and expectations are to be guarded. (3) That it is not safe to base conclusions upon the comparative strength of the friends and enemies of a proposition. (4) That a life that leaves God out rests on a false basis.

FOR STUDY AND DISCUSSION

(1) The rebukes uttered by the prophet. (2) The encouragements he offers. (3) The historical confirmation of the facts of this book found in Ezra. (4) False content and discontent. (5) Basing conclusions upon the comparative strength of the friends and enemies of a proposition, while leaving God out of the count.

CHAPTER XIX

ZECHARIAH AND MALACHI

Lesson 96. Analysis, Introductory Discussions, Messages, topics "For Study and Discussion" and Chapters 1-6 of Zechariah.

Lesson 97. Zechariah, Chs. 9-10 and the book of Malachi, including Analysis, Introductory Discussions, Messages, topics "For Study and Discussion" and Scripture reading.

Lesson 98. Review of Chapter XVI-XIX, Lessons 87-98.

ZECHARIAH

The Prophet. His name means *Remembered of the Lord,* and like Haggai he appears to have been among the captives who returned from Babylon with Zerubbabel. He was a co-laborer with Haggai, beginning his work two months later, and continuing into the second year following him. The conditions of the times were the same as those described in Haggai, and the prophet had the same purpose in mind.

The Prophecy opens with a call of repentance which is followed by eight visions, each of which was calculated to encourage the Jews to finish the temple and rebuild the city and re-establish their old religion and government. The time of the first eight chapters is that of the rebuilding ot the temple, while the remaining chapters, 9-14, are thought to have been written thirty years later. It is distinguished for: The symbolic character of its visions; for the richness of the Messianic predictions found in the second part; and for the large place given to angelic mediation in the intercourse with Jehovah. It is also distinguished by the apocalyptic symbolism that enters into the visions.

The contents have been said to contain: (1) Encouragements to lead the people to repent and reform. (2) Discussions about keeping up the days of fasting and humiliation observed during the captivity. (3) Reflections of a moral and physical nature. (4) Denunciations against some contemporary nations. (5) Promises of the prosperity of God's people. (6) Various predictions concerning Christ and His kingdom.

ANALYSIS

I. Eight Visions Encouraging the Rebuilding of the Temple, Chs. 1-6.

Introduction, 1:1-6.

1. The horseman among the myrtle trees, 1:7-17.
2. The four horns and four carpenters, 1:18-21.
3. The man with the measuring line, Ch. 2.
4. Joshua, the High Priest, and Satan, Ch. 3.
5. The Golden Candlestick, Ch. 4.
6. The Flying Roll, 5:1-4.
7. The woman and the ephah, 5:5-11.
8. The four war chariots, 6:1-8.

Appendix: Joshua crowned as a type of Christ, 6:9-15.

II. Requirement of the Law and the Restoration and Enlargement of Israel, Chs. 7-8.

1. Obedience better than fasting, 7:1-7.
2. Disobedience the source of all their past misery, 7:8-14 end.
3. The restoration and enlargement which prefigure Christ "The Jew," Ch. 8.

III. Visions of the Messianic Kingdom, Chs. 9-14.

1. The Messianic King, Ch. 9-10.
2. The rejected Shepherd, Ch. 11.
3. The restored and penitent people, Chs. 12-13.
4. The divine sovereignty, Ch. 14.

MESSAGES OF ZECHARIAH

(1) That there is a secret guardian of God's people—"The Watcher." (2) That there is a secret supply for God's people—"The olive trees." (3) That certain success will come to God's people in their conflict against their enemies.

FOR STUDY AND DISCUSSION

(1) The symbols and figures used in the several visions. (2) The different ways of expressing or planning the success of God's people and the overthrow of their enemies. (3) The discussion of fasting; should they keep it up? What is superior to it? etc. (4) The promises of these prophecies. (5) The denunciations and judgments found in the book.

MALACHI

The Prophet. His name means *Messenger of the Lord*, or *My Messenger*. He was connected with the reform movement of Nehemiah and Ezra, and condemned the same sins which they condemned. He must, therefore, have lived about 100 years after Haggai and Zechariah, or about 430-420 B. C. He was the last of the Old Testament inspired prophets.

Condition of the Time. The people had been restored to Jerusalem and the temple walls rebuilt. They had become sensual and selfish, and had grown careless and neglectful of their duty. Their interpretation of the glowing prophecies of the exilic and pre-exilic prophets had led them to expect to realize the Messianic kingdom immediately upon their return. They were, therefore, discouraged and grew skeptical (2:17) because of the inequalities of life seen everywhere. This doubt of divine justice had caused them to neglect vital religion, and true piety had given place to mere formality. They had not relapsed into idolatry, but a spirit of worldliness had crept in and they were guilty of many vices such as we see today in professedly Christian communities.

The Prophecy. The purpose of this prophecy was to rebuke the people for departing from the worship of the law of God, to call the people back to Jehovah and to revive their national spirit. He denounced the indifference and hypocrisy of the priests, denounced impure marriages, Sabbath-breaking, the lack of personal godliness, their failure to pay the tithe and their skepticism. There are prophecies of the coming of the Messiah and the characteristics and manner of His coming, and also prophecies concerning the forerunner of the Messiah.

ANALYSIS

Introduction: Jehovah's love of Israel, 1:1-5. This is seen in the contrast between Israel and Edom.

I. Israel's Lack of Love of God, 1:6-2:16. It is proved:

1. By their polluted offerings, 1:6-14 end.
2. By the sins of the priests, 2:1-9.
3. By their heathen marriages and their divorces, 2:10-16.

II. God Will Come and Judge His People, 2:17-4:6.

1. His messenger will separate the righteous from the wicked, 2:17-3:6.
2. This is seen in the effect of their withholding or paying tithes, 3:7-12.
3. Faithful services will be rewarded, 3:13-4:6.

MESSAGES OF MALACHI

(1) That God is the moral governor of the world and that it pays to serve Him. (2) That God's love is unfailing, constant, conscious, and courageous. (3) Concerning human love. All motives but love fail. The death of love makes us fail, and we are powerless without love.

FOR STUDY AND DISCUSSION

(1) Make a list of the particular sins rebuked. (2) Make a list of all the different things said about the Messiah and His mission, and also that of the forerunner. (3) Analyze and study each of the seven controversies, 1:2, 7; 2:13, 14, 17; 3:7, 8, 14. (4) Compare the future destinies of the righteous and wicked as revealed in this book, making a list of all that is said of each. (5) Make a list of all the promises of the book.

CHAPTER XX

MATTHEW AND MARK

Lesson 99. Introductory Discussions and Chs. 1-2 of Matthew.
Lesson 100. Matthew, Chs. 3-7.
Lesson 101. Matthew, Chs. 8-12.
Lesson 102. Matthew, Chs. 13-17.
Lesson 103. Matthew, Chs. 18-23.
Lesson 104. Matthew, Chs. 24-28 and Analysis.
Lesson 105. Introductory Discussion and Ch. 1 of Mark.
Lesson 106. Mark, Chs. 2-6.
Lesson 107. Mark, Chs. 7-11.
Lesson 108. Mark, Chs. 12-16 and Analysis.
Lesson 109. Review on Matthew and Mark with discussion of assigned topics.

MATTHEW

The Gospels. Concerning the four Gospels which we are now about to study, a few facts should be known by all students. (1) They are not a life of Christ. This will be evident when we remember how they almost ignore His childhood and youth; how they give but little of the ordinary, but deal especially with the supernatural in His life and how each left out much that is in the others and no doubt known by the writer. (2) They tell the story of His redemptive work wrought out in His life and death and resurrection. While they do resemble one another, and while each brings certain lessons and information not found in the other, they are entirely separate. Each gospel was written with a view of creating a definite result and was written to a particular people and differs from the others accordingly. In this book each gospel is, therefore, discussed with the hope of so outlining the purpose and consequent peculiarities as to stimulate a thorough study of the questions raised.

Matthew. The author of Matthew always speaks of himself as "the publican," which may indicate his sense of humility, felt in having been exalted from so low an estate to that of an apostle. He was the son of Alphaeus (Mark 2:14; Luke 5:27), and was called Levi until Jesus chose him for an apostle and gave him the name Matthew, which means "Gift of God." We know nothing of his work except his call and farewell feast (9:9-10), and that he was with the apostles on the day of Pentecost. Thus silent, observant and qualified by former occupations, he could well undertake the writing of this book. It might be possible that he was chosen by the others for this great task. We know nothing of his death.

Subject. The Kingdom of God or of Heaven.

Date. Written about 60 A. D., but after Mark.

CHARACTERISTICS AND PURPOSE

1. It Is Not a Chronological but a Systematic and Topical Gospel. There is order in the arrangement of materials so that a definite result may be produced. Materials are treated in groups, as the miracles in chapters eight and nine, and the parables in chapter thirteen. There is order and purpose also in the arrangement of these groups of miracles and parables. The first miracle is the cure of leprosy, and is a type of sin; while the last one is the withering of the fig tree, which is a symbol of judgment. The first parable is that of the seed of the kingdom, which is a symbol of the beginning or planting of the kingdom; the last is that of the talents and prophesies the final adjudication at the last day. The same orderly arrangement is also observed in the two great sections of the book. The first great section, 4:17—16:20, especially sets forth the person and nature of Jesus while the second section, 16:21-27 to the end, narrates His great work for others as seen in His death and resurrection.

2. It is a Didactic or Teaching Gospel. While giving the account of a number of miracles, the book is marked by several discourses of considerable length, as the Sermon on the Mount, chapters 5-7, the denunciation of the Pharisees, chapter 23, the prophecy of the destruction of Jerusalem and the end of the world, chapters 24 and 25, the address to the apostles, chapter 10; and the doctrines of the kingdom, 17:24-20:16. These portions and the parables noted above will indicate how large a portion of the book is taken up in discourse. The student can make lists of other and shorter sections of teaching.

3. It Is a Gospel of Gloom and Despondency. There are no songs of joy like those of Zacharias, Elizabeth, Mary, Simeon, Anna, and the Angels, recorded in Luke. Nor do we see Jesus popular and wise at the age of twelve. Instead, we have his mother almost repudiated and left in disgrace by Joseph and only saved by divine intervention. Jerusalem is in trouble, the male children are killed, and mothers are weeping for them. The child Jesus is saved only by the flight to Egypt. His whole life after the return from Egypt is covered in oblivion and he is a despised Nazarene. The cross is one of desolation, with no penitent thief nor sympathy from anyone, with his enemies reviling, smiting their breasts and passing by. Nor is there much optimism or expectation of success. The disciples are to be rejected and persecuted even as their Lord; many are to be called and but few are chosen; only a few are to find the narrow way; many are to claim entrance into the Kingdom because they have prophesied in His name, but will be denied. Even Matthew himself is a despised and rejected publican.

4. It Is a Kingly Gospel. The genealogy shows the royal descent of Jesus. The Magi came seeking Him that was "born king of the Jews," and John the Baptist preaches that the "kingdom of heaven is at hand." Here we have the parables of the kingdom, beginning with "the kingdom of heaven," etc. In Luke a certain man made a great supper and had two sons, while in Matthew it was a certain king.

In the other evangelists we always have the term "gospel," while, with one exception, Matthew always puts it "the gospel of the kingdom." The "keys of the kingdom" are given to Peter. All the nations shall gather before him as he sits on the throne and "the king says" unto them, and "the king shall answer," etc., (Matt. 25:34-40).

5. **It Is an Official and an Organic Gospel.** This is suggested in that Matthew represents Satan as head of a kingdom; also, in that those connected with Jesus' birth are official persons and most of the acts are official in their nature. Pilate, the judge, washes his hands of the blood of Jesus, the Roman guard pronounces Him the Christ, and the guards say He could not be kept in the tomb. Jesus denounces the officials and calls His own disciples by official names. It is Peter, not Simon, and Matthew, the apostolic name, and not Levi as in Luke. Jesus indicates His official capacity in His rejection of the Jews, telling them that the kingdom is taken away from them (21:43). He makes ready for the establishing of His own kingdom and tells them who is to wield the keys of the kingdom which is not to be bound by time or national relations as was the former kingdom. In Matthew alone do we find full instructions as to the membership, discipline, and ordinances of the church. Here alone are we given in the gospels the command to baptize, to administer the communion, and the beautiful formula for baptism in the name of the Father, Son, and Holy Ghost, and here we have His official command to "Go" backed by all the authority of heaven and earth.

In the further pursuit of this official work, we find Jesus giving especial recognition to the Gentile believers—giving them full place in His kingdom. The genealogy through grace and faith includes Gentiles; the second chapter shows how the Gentile Magi do Him honor; the Roman centurion displays a faith superior to any Israelite; the great faith of the Canaanite woman led Him to heal her daughter, and the Gentile wife of Pilate, because of her dreams, sends a warning that he have "nothing to do" with Him. All this tended to show the official and organic way in which Jesus worked.

6. **It Is a Gospel of Jewish Antagonism and Rejection.** On the one hand the Jews antagonize and reject Jesus. On the other the Jews, especially the Scribes and Pharisees, are exposed and rejected by Jesus. The Pharisees plotted against Jesus and resented His violation of their regulations and customs concerning the Sabbath and their ceremonies about eating and washing and His associations with publicans and sinners. Their opposition culminated in their putting Him to death. On the other hand, Jesus also rejects the Jews. John calls them a generation of vipers and Jesus designated them with such terms as hypocrites, blind guides and whited sepulchres, the climax being reached in chapter 23. It is here that in their wickedness they are unable to discern between the work of God and of Beelzebub. They are told of the application of Isaiah's prophecy, that they have ears and hear not, and that on account of their unworthiness the kingdom is taken from them. The blasting of the fig tree, with which the miracles of Matthew end, show what is to be the fate of the Jewish nation.

7. **It Is a Jewish Gospel.** This is seen in his use of Jewish symbols, terms and numbers without explanation. He never explained the meaning of a Jewish word, such as Corban, nor of a custom, such as to say that the Jews eat not, except they wash. The other evangelists do. He calls Jerusalem by the Jewish terms, "City of the great king," and "Holy City," and Christ, the "Son of David" and the "Son of Abraham." He speaks of the Jewish temple as the temple of God, the dwelling place of God and the holy place. The genealogy is traced to Abraham by three great Jewish events of history. All this would be calculated to win the Jews, but, much more, the sixty-five quotations from the Old Testament and the oft repeated attempt to show that deeds and sayings recorded were that the "Scripture (or saying) might be fulfilled." And, while not seeing as much in the numbers as Plummer and others, one can

hardly believe that all numbers, so characteristic of Jews, are accidental here. The genealogy has three fourteens being multiples of seven. There are fourteen parables, seven in one place and seven in another. There are seven woes in chapter 23. There are twenty miracles separated into two tens. The number seven usually, if not always, divides into four and three, the human and the divine. Of the seven parables in chapter 13, four touch the human or natural, while three refer to the divine or spiritual side of the kingdom. There are seven petitions in the Lord's Prayer, the first three relating to God and the last four to man. A like division is perhaps true in the beatitudes.

ANALYSIS

I. The Beginning of the Kingdom, 1:14-4:16.

1. Jesus, the King, is the Old Testament Messiah, Chs. 1-2.
2. Jesus, the King, is prepared for His work, 3:1-4:16.

II. The Proclamation of the Kingdom, 4:17-16:20.

1. The beginning of the proclamation, 4:17 end.
2. By the sermon on the Mount, Chs. 5-7.
3. By the miracles and connected teachings, Chs. 8-9.
4. By the sending of the Twelve and subsequent teachings and miracles, Chs. 10-12.
5. By seven parables and subsequent miracles, Chs. 8-9.
6. By the denunciation of the Pharisees with attendant miracles and teachings, 15:1-16:12.
7. By the Great Confession, 16:13-20.

III. The Passion of the Kingdom, 16:21-27 end.

1. Four predictions of the passion with intervening discourses and miracles, 16:21-26:2.
   - (a) At Caesarea Philippi, 16:21-17:21.
   - (b) In Galilee near Capernaum, 17:22-20:16.
   - (c) Near Jerusalem, 20:17-22 end.
   - (d) At Jerusalem, 23:1-26:2.
2. The events of the Passion, 26:3-27 end.

IV. The Triumph of the Kingdom, Ch. 28.

1. The resurrection of the King, verses 1-15.
2. Provision for the propagation of the Kingdom, 16-20.

FOR STUDY AND DISCUSSION

(1) Some events of Christ's childhood. (a) The story of the Magi. (b) The massacre of the infants. (c) The flight to Egypt. (d) The return to Nazareth. (2) Two miracles. (a) Two blind men, 9:27-31. (b) Fish with money in its mouth, 17:24-27. (3) Ten Parables. (a) The tares, 13:24-30. (b) The drag net, 13:47-50. (c) The unmerciful servant, 18:23-35. (d) The laborers in the vineyard, 20:1-16. (e) The two sons, 21:28-32. (f) The marriage of the king's son, 22:1-14. (g) The hidden treasure, 13:44. (h) The pearl, 13:45-46. (i) The ten virgins, 25:1-13. (j) The talents, 25:14-30. (4) Ten passages in Christ's discourses. (a) Parts of the Sermon on the Mount, Chaps. 5-7. (b) Revelation to babes, 11:25-27. (c) Invitations to the weary, 11:28-30. (d) About idle words, 12:36-37. (e) Prophecy to Peter, 16:17-19. (f) Humility and forgiveness, 18:15-35. (g) Rejection of the Jews, 21:43. (h) The great denunciation, Chap. 23. (i) The judgment scene, 25:31-46. (j) The great commission and promise, 28:16-20. (5) Some terms by which Jesus is designated in Matthew should be studied. Let the student make a list of the different places where each of the following terms are used and from a study of the passages, compared with any others, form opinions as to the significance of the term: (a) Son of Abraham; (b) Son of David; (c) Son of man; (d) Son of God; (e) Christ, the Christ; f) Jesus; (g) Lord; (h) Kingdom of heaven or Kingdom of God. (6) Make a list of all the places where the expression, "That the saying (or scripture) might be fulfilled" appears and tabulate all the things fulfilled. (7) Show how many times and where the phrase "The Kingdom of Heaven" (or of God) occurs, and from a study of these passages tabulate in list the nature, characteristics and purpose of the Kingdom. (8) Make a list of all the places mentioned and become familiar with the history and geography of each and memorize the leading events connected with each.

MARK

Author. He was not an apostle and was designated in various ways as follows: (1) John, whose surname was Mark, Acts 12:12, 25; 15:37; (2) John only, Acts 13:5, 13; (2) Mark only, Acts 15:39; (4) always Mark after this, Col. 4:10; Philemon 24; II Tim. 4:11; I Peter 5:13. He was a son of Mary, a woman of Jerusalem (Acts 12:12). Her home was the gathering place of the disciples, whither Peter went after he was delivered from prison. On this or some other visit Mark may have been converted through the preaching of Peter, and this may have been the cause of Peter calling him "his son" (I Peter 5:13), which doubtless means son in the ministry. He returns with Paul and Barnabas from Jerusalem to Antioch (Acts 12:25), and accompanies them, as minister (Acts 13:5), on the first great missionary journey as far as Perga (Acts 13:13). There he left them and returned home. On the second missionary tour Paul declined to take him and separated from Barnabas, Mark's cousin (Col. 4:10), who chose Mark for his companion (Acts 15:37-39). Ten years later he seems to be with Paul in his imprisonment at Rome and was certainly counted as a fellow-worker by Paul (Col. 4:10; Philemon 24). Paul found him useful and asked Timothy to bring him to him in his last imprisonment (II Tim. 4:11). He was with Peter when he wrote his first epistle (I Peter 5:13).

What he knew of the work of Jesus directly we do not know, probably not much. The early Christian writers universally say that he was the interpreter for Peter and that he based his gospel upon information gained from him.

Subject. Jesus the Almighty King.

Date. Probably written about A. D. 60, but before Matthew.

CHARACTERISTICS AND PURPOSE

1. It Is a Gospel of Vividness and Detail. He shows the effect of awe and wonder produced upon those present by the works and teaching of Jesus. He relates the details of the actions of Jesus and His disciples and the multitudes. The following will illustrate this: Jesus "looks around," "sat down," "went before;" He is grieved, hungry, angry, indignant; He wonders, sleeps, rests, and is moved with pity; the cock crows twice; "It is the third hour," "A great while before day," or "eventide;" "there are two thousand swine;" the disciples and Jesus are on the sea, on Olivet, in the court yard or in the porch. Everything is portrayed in detail.

2. **It Is a Gospel of Activity and Energy.** There is no story of Jesus' infancy, but Mark starts with, "The beginning of the gospel of Jesus Christ." He portrays the active career of Jesus on earth. He however, lays emphasis upon the works rather than the words of Jesus. Few discourses of any length and only four of the fifteen parables of Matthew are given, and those in the briefest form, while eighteen of the miracles are given in rapid review. The rapid succession is indicated by one Greek word, translated by the seven words, "immediately," "anon," "forthwith," "by and by," "as soon as," "shortly," and "straightway," which occur forty-one times in this gospel. The last meaning, straightway, is truest to the Greek idea, and may be called Mark's characteristic word. It indicates how with the speed of a racer he rushes along and hereby furnishes us a breathless narrative which Farrar says, "makes us 'feel like the apostles,' who, among the press of the people coming and going, were twice made to say they 'had no leisure so much as to eat'." It moves as the scenes of a moving picture show.

3. **It Is a Gospel of Power over Devils.** Here as in no other gospels the devils are made subject to Jesus. They recognize Him as the "Son of God," and acknowledge their subordination to Him as pleading with Him as to what shall be done with them (5:7, 12).

4. It Is a Gospel of Wonder. Everywhere Jesus is a man of wonder that strikes awe and terror and causes to wonder those who see and hear Him. Some of these may be studied, especially in the Greek, in 1:27; 2:12; 4:41; 5:33; 6:50, 51; 7:37. As Archbishop Thompson puts it, "The wonder-working Son of God sweeps over His Kingdom swiftly and meteor-like," and thus strikes awe into the hearts of the onlookers. He is "a man heroic and mysterious, who inspires not only a passionate devotion, but also amazement and adoration."

5. It Is a Gospel for the Romans. The Romans were men of power, mighty workers who left behind them great accomplishments for the blessing of humanity. So that Mark would especially appeal to them by recording of Jesus His mighty deeds. He lets them see One who has power to still the storm, to control disease and death, and even power to control the unseen world of spirits. The Romans, who found deity in a Caesar as head of a mighty Kingdom, would bow to one who had shown himself King in every realm and whose kingdom was both omnipotent and everlasting, both visible and unseen, both temporal and spiritual.

Then, too the Roman cared nothing for Jewish Scripture or prophecy, and so he omits all reference to the Jewish law, the word law not being found in the entire book. He only once or twice refers in any way to the Jewish scriptures. He omits the genealogy of Jesus which could have no value to a Roman. Then, too, he explains all doubtful Jewish words, such as "Boanerges" (3:17), "Talitha cumi" (5:41), "Corban" (7:11). He reduced Jewish money to Roman currency (12:42). He explains Jewish customs and terms as if they were not understood by the readers. (See 7:3; 14:12; 15:42).

And once more by the use of terms familiar to him such as centurion, contend, etc., "Mark showed the Roman a man who was a man indeed." He showed them manhood crowned with glory and power; Jesus of Nazareth, the Son of God; a man but a Man Divine and sinless, among sinful and suffering men. Him, the God-man, no humiliation could degrade, no death defeat. Not even on the cross could He seem less than the King, the Hero, the only Son. And as he gazed on such a picture how could any Roman refrain from exclaiming with the awe-struck centurion, "Truly this was the Son of God."

I. The Almighty King Is Exhibited as the Son of God, 1:1-13.

1. In the baptism and preaching of John, 1-8.
2. In the baptism of Jesus, 9-11.
3. In the temptation, 12:13.

II. The Almighty King at Work in Galilee, 1:14-9 end.

1. Begins His work, 1:14 end.
2. Reveals His kingdom, Chs. 2-5.
3. Meets opposition, 6:1-8:26.
4. Prepares His disciples for the end, 8:27-9 end.

III. The Almighty King Prepares for Death, 10:1-14:31.

1. He goes to Jerusalem, 10:1-11:11.
2. In Jerusalem and vicinity, 11:12-14:31.

IV. The Almighty King Suffers at the Hands of His Enemies, 14:32-15:46.

1. Agony in Gethsemane, 14:32-42.
2. Arrest, 14:43-52.
3. Jewish trial and denial of Peter, 14:53 end.
4. Trial before Pilate, 15:1-15.
5. The crucifixion, 15:16-41.
6. The burial, 15:42-47.

V. The Almighty King Triumphs Over His Enemies, Ch. 16.

1. The resurrection, 1-8.
2. The appearances, 9-18.
3. The ascension, 19-20.

FOR STUDY AND DISCUSSION

(1) Sections peculiar to Mark. (a) Growth of the seed, 4:26-29. (b) Jesus cures the deaf mutes, 7:32-37. (c) The blind man healed gradually, 8:22-26. (d) Details about the ass, etc., 11:1-4. (e) Concerning watching, 13:33-37. (f) De-

tails concerning Christ's appearances, 16:6-11. (2) The spiritual condition of those affected by Jesus' miracles. Keeping in mind their condition before and after the miracle: (a) Were they saved as well as healed? (b) Did they or their friends exercise faith, or did Jesus act voluntarily without any expression of faith? (3) What did Jesus do in performing the miracle? (a) Did He use the touch? (b) Was He touched? (c) Did He simply give command, etc.? (4) From the following scriptures 1:35; 1:45; 3:7-12; 6:6; 6:31-32; 6:46; 7:24-25; 9:2; 11:11; 11:19; 14:1-2, make a list of the different places to which Jesus retired and in connection with each indicate (in writing): (a) Was it before or after a victory or conflict? (b) Was it in preparation for or rest after the performance of a great work? (c) Indicate in each case whether he went alone or was accompanied and, if accompanied, by whom? (d) In each case also tell what Jesus did during the period of retirement. Did He pray, teach, perform miracles or what? (5) List the phrases "Son of man" and "Kingdom of God" and point out the appropriateness and meaning of each. (6) List all references to demons and to demon-oppressed people and study their nature, the nature of their work, their power, wisdom, etc. (7) The facts concerning the death of Jesus, 14:1—15:41. List them.

CHAPTER XXI

LUKE AND JOHN

Lesson 110. Introductory Discussions and Chs. 1-3 of Luke.
Lesson 111. Luke, Chs. 4-10.
Lesson 112. Luke, Chs. 11-17.
Lesson 113. Chs. 18-24 and Analysis.
Lesson 114. Introductory Discussion and Chs. 1-3 of John.
Lesson 115. John, Chs. 4-10.
Lesson 116. John, Chs. 11-16.
Lesson 117. John, Chs. 17-21 and Analysis.
Lesson 118. Review Luke and John, with discussion of assigned topics.

LUKE

Author. The author is Luke, who also wrote Acts. The passages of Acts written in the first person plural, commonly called the "We sections," designate him as one of the companions of Paul. He was with him on his second missionary journey (Acts 16:11-40); joined him at Philippi (Acts 20:1-17) on the return from the third missionary journey, remained with him at Caesarea and accompanied him to Rome (Acts, Chaps. 20-28). He was called the "beloved physician" (Col. 4:14), and Paul's "fellow laborer" (Philemon 24).

From the context of Col. 4:14 we learn that he was "not of the circumcism" and, therefore, a Gentile. From his preface (Luke 1:1) we learn that he was not an eye-witness of what he wrote. He is thought to be "the brother" whose praise is in the gospel throughout all the churches (II Cor. 8:18, and, by tradition, is always declared to be a Gentile and proselyte. As is indicated by the gospel itself, he was the most cultured of all the gospel writers.

Subject. Jesus the World's Savior.

Date. It was probably written about A. D. 60 or 63, certainly before the fall of Jerusalem, A. D. 70, and likely while Luke was with Paul in Rome or during the two years at Caesarea.

CHARACTERISTICS AND PURPOSE

1. It Is a Gospel of Song and Praise. There are a number of songs, such as the song of Mary (1:46-55), the Song of Zacharias, (1:68-79), the song of the angels (2:14), and the song of Simeon (2:29-32). There are many expressions of praise such as 2:20; 5:26; 7:16; 13:13; 17:15; 18:43; 23:47.

2. It Is a Gospel of Prayer. Jesus prays at His baptism (3:21), after cleansing the leper 5:16), before calling the twelve (6:12), at His transfiguration (9:28), before teaching the disciples to pray (11:1), for His murderers as He was on the cross (23:34), with his last breath (23:46). Luke gives us Christ's command to pray (21:36) and two parables, the midnight friend (11:5-13) and the unjust judge (18:1-8) to show the certain and blessed results of continued prayer.

3. It Is a Gospel of Womanhood. No other gospel gives woman anything like so large a place as Luke. Indeed, all of the first three chapters or a greater part of their contents may have been given him, as he "traced out accurately from the first" (1:3), by Mary and Elizabeth. He gives us the praise and prophecy of Elizabeth (1:42-45), the song of Mary (1:46-55), Anna and her worship (2:36-38), sympathy for the widow of Nain (7:12-15), Mary Magdala the sinner (7:36-50), the woman associated with Jesus (8:1-3), tender words to the woman with an issue of blood (8:48), Mary and Martha and their disposition (10:38-42), sympathy and help for the "daughter" of Abraham (13:16), the consolation of the "daughters" of Jerusalem (23:28). These references have been collected by others and are the most conspicuous ones and serve to show how large a place woman is given in this gospel.

4. **It Is a Gospel of the Poor and Outcast.** More than any other of the evangelists, Luke reports those teachings and incidents in the life of our Savior which show how His work is to bless the poor, neglected and vicious. Among the more striking passages of this character are the oft repeated references to the publicans (3:12; 5:27, 29, 30, etc.), Mary Magdala, who was a sinner (7:36-50), the woman with an issue of blood (8:43-48), the harlots (15:30), the prodigal son (15:11-32), Lazarus the beggar (16:19-31), the poor, maimed, halt and blind invited to the supper (14:7-24), the story of Zacchaeus (19:1-9), the Savior's business declared to be to seek and save the lost (19:10), the dying robber saved (23:39-43).

5. **It Is a Gentile Gospel.** The book is everywhere filled with a world-wide purpose not so fully expressed by the other evangelists. Here we have the angels' announcement of great joy which shall be to all people (2:10) and the song about Jesus as "a light for revelation to the Gentiles" (2:32). The genealogy traces Christ's lineage back to Adam (3:38), and thus connects him not with Abraham as a representative of the Jew, but with the first man as a representative of humanity. The fuller account of the sending out of the seventy (10:1-24), the very number of whom signified the supposed number of the heathen nations, who were to go, not as the twelve to the lost sheep of the house of Israel, but to all those cities whither Jesus Himself would come, is suggestive of this broader purpose of Luke. The good Samaritan (10:25-37) is Christ's illustration of a true neighbor and in some way also intends to show the nature of Christ's work which was to be without nationality. Of the ten lepers healed (17:11-19) only one, a Samaritan, returned to render Him praise, thus showing how others than the Jews would not only be blessed by Him but would do worthy service for Him. The Perean

ministry, across the Jordan (9-51—18:4, probably 9:51—19:28), is a ministry to the Gentiles and shows how large a place Luke would give the Gentiles in the work and blessings of Jesus.

6. **It Is a Gospel for the Greeks.** If Matthew wrote for Jews and Mark for Romans, it is but natural that some one should write in such a way as to appeal, specially, to the Greeks as the other representative race. And, such the Christian writers of the first centuries thought to be Luke's purpose. The Greek was the representative of reason and humanity and felt that his mission was to perfect humanity. "The full-grown Greek would be a perfect world man," able to meet all men on the common plane of the race. All the Greek gods were, therefore, images of some form of perfect humanity. The Hindu might worship an emblem of physical force, the Roman deify the Emperor, and the Egyptian any and all forms of life, but the Greek adored man with his thought and beauty of speech, and, in this, had most nearly approached the true conception of God. The Jew would value men as the descendants of Abraham; the Roman according as they wielded empires, but the Greek on the basis of man as such.

The gospel for the Greek must, therefore, present the perfect man, and so Luke wrote about the Divine Man as the Savior of all men. Christ touched man at every point and is interested in him as man whether low and vile or high and noble. By His life He shows the folly of sin and the beauty of holiness. He brings God near enough to meet the longings of the Greek soul and thereby furnishes him a pattern and brother suited for all ages and all people. The deeds of Jesus are kept in the background while much is made of the songs of others and the discourses of Jesus as they were calculated to appeal to the cultured Greek. If the Greek thinks he has a mission to humanity, Luke opens a mission ground enough for the present and offers him an immortality that will satisfy in the future.

7. It Is an Artistic Gospel. Renan calls Luke the most beautiful book in the world, while Dr. Robertson says, "the charm and style and the skill in the use of facts place it above all praise." The delicacy and accuracy, picturesqueness and precision with which he sets forth the different incidents are manifestly the work of a trained historian. His is the most beautiful Greek and shows the highest touches of culture of all the gospels.

ANALYSIS

Introduction. The dedication of the gospel, 1:1-4.

I. The Savior's Manifestation, 1:5-4:13.

1. The announcement of the Forerunner, 1:5-25.
2. The announcement of the Savior, 1:26-38.
3. The Thanksgiving of Mary and Elizabeth, 1:39-56.
4. The birth and childhood of the Forerunner, 1:57 end.
5. The birth of the Savior, 2:1-20.
6. The childhood of the Savior, 3:1-4:13.

II. The Savior's Work and Teaching in Galilee, 4:14-9:50.

1. He preaches in the synagogue at Nazareth, 4:14-30.
2. He works in and around Capernaum, 4:31-6:11.
3. Work while touring Galilee, 6:12-9:50.

III. The Savior's Work and Teaching after Leaving Galilee up to the Entrance into Jerusalem, 9:51-19:27.

1. He journeyed to Jerusalem, 9:51 end.
2. The mission of the seventy and subsequent matters, 10:1-11:13.
3. He exposes the experience and practice of the day, 11:14-12 end.
4. Teachings, miracles, warnings and parables, 13:1-18:30.
5. Incidents connected with His final approach to Jerusalem, 18:31-19:27.

IV. The Savior's Work and Teaching in Jerusalem, 19:28-22:38.

1. The entrance into Jerusalem, 19:28 end.
2. Questions and answers, Ch. 20.
3. The widow's mites, 21:1-4.
4. Preparation for the end, 21:5-22:38.

V. The Savior Suffers for the World, 22:39-23 end.

1. The agony in the garden, 22:39-46.
2. The betrayal and arrest, 22:47-53.
3. The trial, 22:54-23:26.
4. The cross, 23:27-49.
5. The burial, 23:50 end.

VI. The Savior Is Glorified, Ch. 24.

1. The resurrection, 1-12.
2. The appearance and teachings, 13-49.
3. The ascension, 50 end.

FOR STUDY AND DISCUSSION

1. Six Miracles Peculiar to Luke: (1) The draught of fishes 5:4-11. (2) The raising of the widow's son, 7:11-17. (3) The woman with the spirit of infirmity, 13:11-17. (4) The man with the dropsy, 14:1-6. (5) The ten lepers, 17:11-19. (6) The healing of Malchus' ear, 22:50-51.

2. Eleven Parables Peculiar to Luke: (1) The two debtors, 7:41-43. (2) The good Samaritan, 10:25-37. (3) The importunate friend, 11:5-8. (4) The rich fool, 12:16-21. (5) The barren fig tree, 13:6-9. (6) The lost piece of silver, 15:8-10. (7) The prodigal son, 15:11-32. (8) The unjust steward, 16:1-13. (9) The rich man and Lazarus, 16:19-31. (10) The unjust judge, 18:1-8. (11) The Pharisee and publican, 18:9-14.

3. Some Other Passages Mainly Peculiar to Luke: (1) Chaps. 1 and 2 and 9:51-18:14 are mainly peculiar to Luke. (2) John the Baptist's answer to the people, 3:10-14. (3) The conversation with Moses and Elias, 9:30-31. (4) The weeping over Jerusalem, 19:41-44. (5) The bloody sweat, 22:44. (6) The sending of Jesus to Herod, 23:7-12. (7) The address to the daughters of Jerusalem, 23:27-31. (8) "Father forgive them," 23:34. (9) The penitent robber, 23:40-43. (10) The disciples at Emmaus, 24:13-31. (11) Particulars about the ascension, 24:50-53.

4. The Following Words and Phrases Should be Studied, making a list of the references where each occurs and a study of each passage in which it occurs with a view of getting Luke's conception of the terms: (1) The "Son of man" (23 times). (2) The "Son of God" (7 times). (3) The "kingdom of God" 32 times). (4) References to law, lawyer, lawful (18 times). (5) Publican (11 times). (6) Sinner and sinners (16 times). Mr. Stroud estimates that 59 per cent of Luke is peculiar to himself, and Mr. Weiss figures that 541 verses have no coincidences in the other gospels.

JOHN

Author. From the evidence found in the gospel, we may learn several things about the author. 1) *That he was a Jew.* This is seen in his evident knowledge of Jewish opinions concerning such subjects as the Messiah, and his knowledge of their customs, such as the purification. (2) *He was an eye - witness to most of what he relates.* This is seen in his exact knowledge of time, as to the hour or time of day a thing occurred; in his knowledge of the number of persons or things present, as the division of His garments into four parts; in the vividness of the narrative which he could hardly have had without first having seen it all. (3) *He was an apostle.* This is seen in his knowledge of the thoughts of the disciples (2:11, 17); in his knowledge of the private words of the disciples to Jesus and among themselves (4:31, 33, etc.); in his knowledge of the private resorts of the disciples (11:54, etc.); in his knowledge of the Lord's motives, etc. (2:24-25, etc.); and in his knowledge of Christ's feelings (11:33). (4) *He was the son of Zebedee* (Mar. 1:19-20), and was probably one of John's two disciples whom he turned to Jesus (1:40). (5) *He is one of the three most prominent of the apostles,* being several times especially honored (Matt. 17:1-3, etc.), and is prominent in the work of the church after Christ's ascension, as well as in all the work before his death. (6) *He also wrote three epistles and Revelation.* He outlived all the other apostles and is supposed to have died on the Isle of Patmos as an exile about 100 A. D.

Time and Circumstances of the Writing. These are so different from those which influenced the other evangelists that one can hardly escape the feeling that John's gospel is colored accordingly. The gospel had been preached in all the Roman empire and Christianity was no longer considered a Jewish sect, attached to the synagogue. Jerusalem had been overthrown and the temple destroyed. Christianity had been sorely persecuted, but had achieved great triumphs in many lands. All the rest of the New Testament except Revelation had been written. Some had arisen who disputed the deity of Jesus and, while the gospel is not a mere polemic against the false teachings, it does, by establishing the true preaching, thoroughly undermine the false. He perhaps wrote to Christians of all nationalities, whose history had by this time been enriched by the blood of martyrs for the faith. Instead of the Messiah in whom Jews would find a Savior, or the Mighty Worker in whom the Romans would find Him, or the Ideal Man in whom the Greeks would find Him, John wrote concerning the Eternal, Incarnate Word in whose spiritual kingdom each, having lost his narrowness and racial prejudice, could be forever united.

Style and Plan—This gospel differs from the others in language and plan. It is both profound and simple and has several elements of style as follows: (1) *Simplicity.* The sentences are short and connected by co-ordinate conjunctions. There are but few direct quotations, and but few dependent sentences, and most of them show the sequence of things, either as a cause or a purpose. (2) *Sameness.* This arises from the method of treating each step in the narrative as if isolated and separate from all the rest rather than merging it into the complete whole. (3) *Repetition,* whether in the narrative proper or in the quoted words of the Lord, is very frequent. The following examples will illustrate this: "In the beginning was the word and the word was with God and the word was God." "The light shineth in darkness and the darkness comprehendeth it not." "I am the Good Shepherd; the Good Shepherd giveth life." "Jesus then, when He saw her weeping and the Jews that were weeping with her." "If I bear witness of myself my witness is not true. There is another that beareth witness of me; and I know that the witness which He witnessed of me is true." Let the student gather a list of all such repetitions. (4) *Parallelisms* or statements expressing the same or similar truths, such as the following, are common: "Peace I leave with you, my peace I give unto you"; "Let not your heart be troubled, neither let it be afraid"; "I give unto them eternal life and they shall never perish." This parallelism, which at the same time becomes a repetition, is seen in the way a subject or conclusion is stated and, after elaboration, restated in a new and enlarged view, thus teaching the truth in gradually unfolding beauty and force. An illustration is found in the statement, "I will raise him up in the last day," (6:39, 40, 44). (5) *Contrasts.* The plan is more simple and more easily seen all along than is that of any other of the evangelists. On the one hand, he shows how love and faith are developed in the believer until, in the end, Thomas, who was the most doubtful of all, could exclaim, "My Lord and my God." On the other hand, he shows how the unbeliever advanced from mere indifference to a positive hatred that culminated in the crucifixion. This purpose is carried out by a process of contrasting and separating things that are opposites, such as (a) Light and darkness, (b) truth and falsehood, (c) good and evil, (d) life and death, (e) God and Satan. In all of these he is convincing his reader that Jesus is the Christ, the Son of God.

Subject. Jesus, the Christ, God's Son.

Date. Perhaps between A. D. 85 and 95.

CHARACTERISTICS AND PURPOSE

1. It Is a Gospel of the Feasts. Indeed, if we subtract from it those miracles and teachings and other works performed in connection with the feasts, we should have only a few fragments left. The value of the book would be destroyed, and the most beautiful and profound teachings of the gospel lost.

The student will do well from the following list of feasts to endeavor to group around each all that John records as occurring in connection with it. (1) The Feast of the Passover (2:13, 23), First Passover, A. D. 27. (2) A Feast of the Jews (5:1) probably Purim. (3) Passover, a Feast of the Jews (6:4), Second Passover, A. D. 28. (4) Feast of the Tabernacles (7:2). (5) Feast of the Dedication (10:22). (6) Passover (11:55, 56; 12:1, 12, 20; 13:2-30, 18:28), Third Passover, A. D. 29.

2. It Is a Gospel of Testimony. John writes to prove that Jesus is the Christ. He assumes the attitude of a lawyer before a jury and introduces testimony until he feels certain of his case and then closes the testimony with the assurance that much more could be offered if it seemed necessary. There are seven lines of testimony: (1) The testimony of John the Baptist. (2) The testimony of certain other individuals. (3) The testimony of Jesus' work. (4) The testimony of Jesus to Himself (see the I am's). (5) The testimony of the scripture. (6) The testimony of the Father. (7) The testimony of the Holy Spirit.

3. It Is a Gospel of Belief. The writer states distinctly (20:30, 31) that it is his purpose in writing to lead the people to believe in Jesus. In trying to accomplish this purpose he gives numerous examples of those who believe. He also announces many teachings concerning belief. In these examples and teachings, he shows us how faith may grow; its secret or basis, such as hearing and receiving the word, and its results such as freedom, rest, peace, power, eternal life, etc.

4. It Is the Spiritual Gospel. It represents the deeper meditations of John, which are so shaped as to establish a great doctrine which, instead of history, becomes his great impulse. To John "history is doctrine," and he reviews it in the light of its spiritual interpretation. It furnishes a great bulwark against the Gnostic teachers, who had come to deny the deity of Jesus. He also emphasized and elaborated the humanity of Jesus. His whole purpose is "not so much the historic record of the facts as the development of their inmost meaning."

5. It Is a Gospel of Symbolism. John was a mystic and delighted in mystic symbols. The whole book speaks in the language of symbols. The mystic numbers, three and seven, prevail throughout the book, not only in what is recorded, but in the arrangement of topics. Each of the eight miracles is used for a "sign" or symbol, as the feeding of the five thousand in which Jesus appears as the bread or support of life. The significant passages on the Good Shepherd, the sheep-fold, and the vine; the several names employed designating Jesus as the Word, the Way, the Light, the Truth, the Life, etc., show how the entire Gospel is penetrated by a spirit of symbolic representation.

6. It Is the Gospel of the Incarnation. "Matthew explains his Messianic function; Mark his active work, and Luke his character as Savior." John magnifies His person and everywhere makes us see "the word made flesh." God is at no great distance from us. He has become flesh. The word has come as the Incarnate Man. Jesus, this Incarnate Man, is God and as such fills the whole book, but He, nevertheless, hungers, thirsts, and knows human experience. God has come down to man that man may be enabled to ascend to God; to enable him to rise up to God.

ANALYSIS

Introduction or Prologue, 1:1-18.

1. **The divine nature of the Word, 1-5.**
2. **The manifestation of the Word as the world's Savior, 6-18.**

I. The Testimony of His Great Public Ministry, 1:9-12 end.

1. He is revealed, 1:19-2:12.
2. He is recognized, 2:13-4 end.
3. He is antagonized, Chs. 5-11.
4. He is honored, Ch. 12.

II. The Testimony of His Private Ministry with His Disciples, Chs. 13-17.

1. He teaches and comforts His disciples, Chs. 13-16.
2. He prays for His disciples, Ch. 17.

III. The Testimony of His Passion, Chs. 18-19.

1. His betrayal, 18:1-11.
2. The Jewish or ecclesiastical trial, 18:12-27.
3. The roman or civil trial, 18:28-19:16.
4. His death and burial, 19:17 end.

IV. The Testimony of His Resurrection and Manifestation, Chs. 20-21.

1. His resurrection and manifestation to His disciples, Ch. 20.
2. Further manifestation and instruction to His disciples, Ch. 21.

FOR STUDY AND DISCUSSION

(1) The events and discourses connected with each feast mentioned above. (2) The seven lines of testimony mentioned above. List examples of each. (3) The following miracles as "signs," pointing out what they symbolize about Jesus: (a) The Cana miracle, 2:1-11. (b) The nobleman's son, 4:48-54. (c) The impotent man, 5:1-16. (d) Feeding five thousand, 6:3-14. (e) Walking on the sea, 6:16-20. (f) Healing the blind man, 9:1-16. Read all the chapter. (g) Raising Lazarus, Chap. 11. (h) The draft of fishes, 21:1-11. (4) The following discourses: (a) The conversation with Nicodemus, Chap. 3. (b) The conversation with the woman at the well, Chap. 4. (c) The discourse on the shepherd and the sheep, Chap. 10. (d) The discussion of Chapter 13. (e) The discourse on the vine, Chap. 15. (f) The Lord's Prayer, Chap. 17. (5) From the following passages find the cause or explanation of unbelief: 1:46, 3:11, 19, 20; 5:16, 40, 42, 44; 6:42, 52; 7:41, 42, 48; 8:13, 14, 15; 20:9.

(6) From the following study the results of unbelief: 3:18, 20, 36; 4:13, 14; 6:35, 53, 58; 8:19, 34, 55; 14:1, 28; 15:5; 16:6, 9. (7) Make a list of all the night scenes of the book and study them. (8) Study each instance of some one worshiping Jesus. (9) Name each chapter of the book so as to indicate some important event in it—as the Vine chapter or Good Shepherd chapter. (10) Find where and how many times each of the following words and phrases occur and study them as time will admit. (1) Eternal life, 17 times, only 18 times in all the other gospels; (2) believe; (3) believe on; (4) sent; (5) life; (6) sign or signs (Revised Version); (7) Work or works; (8) John the Baptist; (9) verily, always double and used by Jesus; (10) receive, received, etc.; (11) witness, or testify, testimony, etc.; (12) truth; (13) manifest, manifested; (14) "I am" (spoken by Jesus).

CHAPTER XXII

ACTS AND ROMANS

Lesson 119. Introductory Discussions and Chs. 1-15 of Acts.
Lesson 120. Acts, Chs. 6-12.
Lesson 121. Acts, Chs. 13-18.
Lesson 122. Acts, Chs. 19-25.
Lesson 123. Acts, Chs. 26-28, Analysis and review of Acts with the discussion of assigned topics.
Lesson 124. Introductory Discussions and Chs. 1-4 of Romans.
Lesson 125. Romans, Chs. 5-11.
Lesson 126. Romans, Chs. 12-16, Analysis and topics "For Study and Discussion."

ACTS

Author. The author is Luke who wrote the gospel of Luke. Facts concerning him may be found in chapter twenty of our text which discusses the book of Luke. He wrote this book about A. D. 63 or 64.

Purpose. It was addressed to an individual as a sort of continuation of the former treatise and aims to chronicle the growth and development of the movement inaugurated by Jesus as it was carried on by the apostles after the resurrection and ascension of Jesus. It is taken up largely with the history of Christian work among the Gentiles and only gives enough of the history of the Jerusalem church to authenticate the work among the Gentiles. The chief purpose, therefore, seems to be to give an account of the spread of Christianity among the Gentiles. This view is further strengthened by the fact that Luke himself was a Gentile (Col. 4:10) and that he was a companion of Paul (Col. 4:14) and the "We" sections of Acts. The book does not therefore, claim to be a complete account of the labors of the early apostles. But it does give in a simple, definite, and impressive manner an account of how the religion of Jesus was propagated after His death, and how it was received by those to whom it was first preached. It tells something of the earliest persecutions of Christians, of the first martyrs, and of the first Gentile converts, but it omits any discussion of a number of the Apostles, of the later ministry of Peter, and much concerning Paul's experiences on his missionary journeys. During recent years many discoveries have been made that show that Luke was careful and exact in his details about geographical positions and accurate in his knowledge of political conditions.

Spirituality. In the Old Testament God the Father was the active agent. In the gospels God the Son (Jesus) was the active agent. In Acts (and even after) God the Holy Spirit is the active agent. He is mentioned about seventy times in Acts. The Savior had told the apostles to wait at Jerusalem for the power of the Holy Ghost. Until they were endued with His power they were very ordinary men. Afterward they were pure in their purpose and ideals, and were always triumphant in their cause. The book is a record of mighty spiritual power seen in action everywhere.

ANALYSIS

Introduction, 1:1-3.

I. The Church Witnessing in Jerusalem, 1:4-8:1.

1. Preparation for witnessing, 1:4-2:4.
2. First witnessing, 2:5-47.
3. First persecution, 3:1-4:31.
4. Blessed state of the church, 4:32-5:42.
5. First deacons, 6:1-7.
6. The first martyr, 6:8-8:1.

II. The Church Witnessing in Palestine, 8:2-12:25.
1. The witnesses are scattered abroad, 8:2-4.
2. Philip witnesses in Samaria and Judea, 8:5-40.
3. The Lord wins new witnesses, 9:1-11:18.
4. Center of labor changed to Antioch, 11:19-30.
5. The witnesses triumph over Herod's persecution, 12:1-25.

III. The Church Witnessing to the Gentile World, 13:1-28:31.
1. Witnessing in Asia, Chs. 13:14. — Paul's First Missionary Journey.
2. The first church council, 15:1-35.
3. Witnessing in Europe, 15:36-18:22. — Paul's Second Missionary Journey.
4. Further witnessing in Asia and Europe, 18:23-21:17. — Paul's Third Missionary Journey.
5. Paul, the witness, rejected and attacked by the Jews at Jerusalem, 21:18-23:35.
6. Two year's imprisonment at Caesarea, Chs. 24-26.
7. Paul, the witness, carried to Rome, 27:1-28:15.
8. Paul, the witness, at Rome, 28:16-31.

FOR STUDY AND DISCUSSION

(1) The first church conference for business, 1:15-26. (2) The coming of the Holy Spirit, 2:1-4. (3) Peter's sermon on the day of Pentecost, 2:5-47. (4) The first miracle, Chap. 3. (5) The first persecution, 4:1-31. (6) Death of Ananias and Sapphira, 5:1-11. (7) The first deacons, 6:1-7. (8) The first martyr, Chap. 7. (9) Philip's work in Samaria, 8:5-40. (10) Conversion of Saul, 9:1-31. (11) Conversion of Cornelius, 10:1—11:18. (12) List the principal churches of the book, their location, and what makes them notable. (13) List the principal preachers of the book and note the sermons or miracles, etc., that make them prominent. (14) The sermons and addresses of the book, to whom and by whom each was delivered, its purpose, etc. (15) The chief elements of power of these early disciples (16) The growth of Christianity and the hindrances it had to overcome. (17) The great outstanding teachings of these early Christians. (18) The tact and adaptation of the apostles (give examples). (19) The different plans to kill

Paul and the ways by which he escaped each. (20) The missionary journeys of Paul and his journey to Rome as a prisoner.

ROMANS

Author. Paul, the author, was a Hebrew by descent, a native of Tarsus in Cilicia, and educated by Gamaliel, the great Pharisaic teacher. He was one of the most unmerciful persecutors of the early Christians, but was converted by the sudden appearance to him of the risen Lord. He began preaching at Damascus, but on account of persecution went into Arabia. Returning from Arabia he visited Jerusalem and Damascus, and then went to Cilicia, where he doubtless did evangelistic work until Barnabas sought him at Tarsus and brought him to Antioch, where he worked a year with Barnabas. After this they went to Jerusalem with contributions for the brethren. Upon his return to Antioch he was called by the Holy Ghost to mission work in which he continued till his death, making at least three great missionary journeys, during which and afterward he suffered "one long martydom" till his death as a martyr.

Paul's Epistles. Paul's epistles are commonly put into four groups as follows: (1) *The Eschatological group,* or those dealing with the second coming of Christ. These are I and II Thessalonians and were written from Corinth about 62 or 63 A. D. (2) *The Anti-Judaic group,* or those growing out of controversy with Judaistic teachers. They are I Corinthians, II Corinthians, Galatians, and Romans, written during the third Missionary journey, probably at Ephesus, Philippi, and Corinth. (3) *The Christological group,* which center their teachings around the character and work of Jesus, and were written during the imprisonment at Rome. They are Philippians, Colossians, Philemon, Ephesians, and Hebrews (many think Paul did not write Hebrews). (4) *The Pastoral group,* or those written to young preachers touching matters of church organization and government and practical instructions concerning evangelists, pastors, and other Christian workers. They are I Timothy, II Timothy and Titus.

All of Paul's Epistles, unless it be Hebrews, fall very naturally into five sections, as follows: (1) *An Introduction,* which may contain a salutation, usually including the subject of the epistle and the names of those with Paul as co-laborers at the time of the writing, and a thanksgiving for the good character or conduct of those whom he addresses. (2) *A Doctrinal Section,* in which he discusses some great Christian teachings, which needs special emphasis in the case of the church or individual addressed. (3) *A Practical Section,* in which he sets forth the practical application of the principles discussed in the doctrinal section to the life of those addressed. (4) *A Personal Section,* in which are personal messages and salutations sent to and by various friends. (5) *A Conclusion,* in which may be found a benediction or autograph conclusion to authenticate the letter, maybe both, with other closing words.

Occasion of the Roman Epistle. (1) Paul longed to go to Rome (Acts 19:21) and now hoped soon to do so (Romans 15:24-33). He may, therefore, have wished them to know of his doctrine before his arrival, especially as they had perhaps heard some false reports of it. (2) It was just after he wrote Galatians and Paul's mind was full of the doctrine of justification, and he may have desired to write further upon the subject, giving special emphasis to the divine side of the doctrine as he had given to the human side of it in Galatians. (3) Then, too, he may have been misunderstood in Galatians and desired to enlarge upon his teaching. In Galatians man is justified by believing; in Romans God gives His own righteousness to the believer for his justification. (4) Phoebe, a woman of influence and Christian character, a friend of Paul, was about to go to Rome from the coasts of Corinth, and Paul not only had a good opportunity to send the letter, but could do her a service by way of introducing her (16:1-2).

The Church at Rome. It was doubtless in a very prosperous condition at the time of Paul's writing. It was perhaps organized by some Jews who heard and believed while at Jerusalem, probably on the day of Pentecost. While its membership included both Jews and Gentiles (1:6-13), it was regarded by Paul especially as a Gentile church (1:5-7, 13-15).

Some Errors of Doctrine and Practice Had Crept in which Needed Correction. (1) They seemed to have misunderstood Paul's teachings and to have charged that he taught that the greater the sin the greater the glory of God (3:8). (2) They may have thought him to teach that we should sin in order to get more grace (6:1) and, therefore, may have made his teaching of justification by faith an excuse for immoral conduct. (3) The Jews would not recognize the Gentile Christian as equal with them in Christ's Kingdom. Some of the Gentile brethren, on the other hand, looked with contempt upon their narrow and prejudiced and bigoted Jewish brethren (14:3). (5) Paul, therefore, aimed to win the Jews to Christian truth and the Gentiles to Christian love.

Paul's Connection with the Church. He had never been there up to this time (1:11, 13, 15) and it is not likely that any other apostle had been there. For if other apostles had already been there, Paul would not have been planning to go, since his rule was not to go where another had worked (15:20; II Cor. 10:14-16). This strikes a heavy blow at Catholicism's claim that Peter was first bishop of Rome. If Paul would not have followed him, then Peter had not been there, and the most important test of papacy is overthrown. Paul had, however, many intimate friends and acquaintances at Rome, many of whom were mentioned in chapter 16. Among them were his old friends, Aquilla and Priscilla.

Argument of the Book. The doctrines of the book are considered and discussed under four main propositions: (1) All men are guilty before God (Jews and Gentiles alike). (2) All men need a Savior. (3) Christ died for all men. (4) We all, through faith, are one body in Christ.

Date. Probably from Corinth, about A. D. 58.

Theme. The gift of the righteousness of God as our justification which is received through faith in Christ, or justification by faith.

ANALYSIS

Introduction, 1:1-17.

I. All Men Need Righteousness, 1:18-3:20.

II. All Men May Have Righteousness by Faith in Christ (justification), 3:21-4 end.

III. All Who Are Thus Justified Will Be Finally Sanctified, Chs. 5-8. The believer's final redemption is thus guaranteed.

1. By the new relation to God which this righteousness gives, Ch. 5.
2. By the new realms of grace into which it brings him, Ch. 6. (no death in this realm).
3. By the new nature given him, Ch. 7. This wars against the old nature and will win.
4. By the new possession (the Holy Spirit) which it gives, Ch. 8:1-27.
5. By the foreordained purpose of God for them, 8:28-39.

IV. This Doctrine as Related to the Rejection of the Jews, Chs. 9-11.

1. The justice of their rejection, 9:1-29.
2. The cause of their rejection, 9:30-10 end.
3. The limitations of their rejection, Ch. 11.

V. The Application of This Doctrine to Christian Life, 12:1-15:13.

1. Duty to God—consecration, 12:1-2.
2. Duty to self—a holy life, 12:3 end.
3. Duty to state authorities—honor, 13:1-7.

4. Duty to society—love all, 13:8-10.
5. Duty as to the Lord's return—watchfulness, 13:11-14.
6. Duty to the weak—helpfulness and forbearance, 14:1-15:13.

Conclusion, 15:14-16 end. (1) Personal matters, 15:14 end. (2) Farewell greetings and warnings, Ch. 16.

FOR STUDY AND DISCUSSION

(1) The greeting (1:1-7) what does it reveal about (a) The call, duty, and standing of an apostle or preacher? (b) The standing, privileges, and duties of a church, or individual Christian? (c) The relation of the old dispensation to the new? (d) Christ's deity or His Messiahship in fulfilment of prophecy? (e) The different persons of the Trinity? (2) Study sin as described in 3:10-18, and what can be learned concerning: (a) The state of sin (b) The practice of sin (c) The reason for sin. (3) Abraham as an example of justification by faith, Chap. 4. (4) The plan and method by which God rescues men from sin, 5:6-11. (5) The contrast between Adam and Christ, 5:12-31. Do we get more in Christ than we lost in Adam? (6) Why a man under grace should not continue in sin, 6:1-14. (7) A converted man's relation to the law, 7:1-6. (8) The different things done for us by the Holy Spirit, 8:1-27. (9) The practical duties of a Christian, Chap. 12. (10) Make a list of the following "key-words," showing how many times and where each occurs, and outline from the Scripture references the teachings about each. Power, sin, and unrighteousness, righteousness, justification, faith and belief, atonement, redemption, adoption, propitiation, election, predestination.

CHAPTER XXIII

FIRST AND SECOND CORINTHIANS

Lesson 127. Analysis, Introductory Discussion and Chs. 1-5 of First Corinthians.

Lesson 128. First Corinthians, Chs. 6-12.

Lesson 129. First Corinthians, Chs. 13-16, and Analysis, Introductory Discussion and Chs. 1-2 of II Corinthians.

Lesson 130. Second Corinthians, Chs. 3-9.

Lesson 131. Second Corinthians, Chs. 10-13, and reviews of Romans and First and Second Corinthians.

FIRST CORINTHIANS

The City of Corinth. It contained 400,000 inhabitants and was the chief city of Greece when Paul visited it, being situated on a large isthmus, where the commerce of the world passed. The inhabitants were Greeks, Jews, Italians, and a mixed multitude from everywhere. Sailors, merchants, adventurers, and refugees from all the world crowded the city, bringing with them the evils of every country, out of which grew many forms of human degradation. The various arts were encouraged, the city was embellished, and the temples were adorned. Here the Corinthian style of architecture originated, and the Isthmian games were held here biennially. By the end of the second century of our era it had become one of the richest if not the richest city in the world. Religion and philosophy had been prostituted to low uses. Intellectual life was put above moral life, and the future life was denied that they might enjoy the present life without restraint.

The Church at Corinth. It was founded by Paul on the second missionary journey (Acts 18:1-8). His spirit in founding the church is seen in I Cor. 2:1, 2. While there Paul made his home with Aquila and Priscilla, Jews who had been expelled from Rome (Acts 18:2, 3), but who now became members of the church. Apollos preached to this church and aided it in Paul's absence (18:24-28; 19:1). Both epistles are full of information as to the condition of the church and the many problems which it had to face from time to time. It must be remembered that Corinth was one of the most wicked cities of ancient times, and that the church was surrounded by heathen customs and practices. Many of its members had but recently been converted from heathenism to Christianity and the church was far from ideal. There were among them true Christians who were ideal in their Christian faith and character (1:4-8). But they were for the most part poor and without pride of birth or learning (1:26). But the problem of adjustment was very difficult. They must meet every form of philosophical question as well as every kind of evil practice. They were blazing the way for us while Christianity was having its greatest test of all times.

Occasion and Purpose of First Corinthians. Unfavorable news had come to Paul concerning the Corinthian church and he had written them a letter (5:9) which had been lost. In that letter he seems to have commanded them to give up their evil practices and promised to visit them. In the meantime, members of the household of Chloe (1:11) and other friends (16:17) came to him at Ephesus and brought news of their divisions and of the evil practices of certain of their members. Finally, they wrote him a letter asking his advice on certain matters (7:1). From all this we learn (1) that there were four factions among them (1:12); (2) that there was gross immorality in the church as in the case of the incestuous person, Chap. 5; (3) that they went to law with each other, Chap. 6; (4) that many practical matters troubled them. Paul, therefore, wrote to correct all these errors in doctrine and practice.

Content of First Corinthians. This letter contains some of the greatest passages in the New Testament. It is, however, remarkable, especially for the very practical nature of its contents. It deals with many of the problems of everyday life and has been said to discuss but one great doctrine, that of the resurrection.

Date. From Ephesus, in the spring of A. D. 57.

ANALYSIS

Introduction, 1:1-9.

I. **Concerning Divisions and the Party Spirit,** 1:10-4 end.

Divisions are prevented:

1. By Christ as the center of Christianity, 1:10 end.
2. By spiritual mindedness, 2:1-3:4.
3. By a right view of preachers, 3:5-4 end.

II. **Correction of Moral Disorders,** Chs. 5-6.

1. The incestuous person, Ch. 5.
2. Lawsuits, 6:1-11.
3. Sins of the body, 6:12 end.

III. **Answers to Questions and Cognate Matters,** 7:1-16:4.

1. Concerning marriage and celibacy, Ch. 7.
2. Concerning things offered to idols, 8:1-11:1.
3. Concerning head dress, 11:1-6.
4. Concerning the Lord's Supper, 11:17 end.
5. Concerning spiritual gifts, Chs. 12-14.
6. Concerning the resurrection, Ch. 15.
7. Concerning collections for the saints, 16:1-4.

IV. **Personal Matters and Conclusions,** 16:5 end.

FOR STUDY AND DISCUSSION

(1) Earthly wisdom and heavenly foolishness, 1:18-25. (2) Spiritual wisdom, 2:7-16. (3) Paul's apostolic labors, 4:9-13. (4) The Scripture estimate of the human body, 6:12-20. (5) Marriages and divorce, 7:25-40, letting "virgin" mean any single person, male or female. (6) Paul's

practice in the matter of his rights, 9:1-23. (7) The Christian race, 9:24-27. (8) Love and its nature, Chap. 13. (a) Superior to other gifts, 1-3; (b) Its ten marks, 4-6; (c) Its power, 7; (d) Its performance, 8-13. (9) Spiritual gifts, Chaps. 12-14. Name and describe them. 10) The resurrection, Chap. 15. (a) Calamities to result, if there were none—or the other doctrines here made to depend on the resurrection; (b) The nature of the resurrected body.

SECOND CORINTHIANS

Occasion and Purpose of the Letter. From suggestions found here and there in these two epistles it appears that much communication passed between Paul and the church, and that the two letters that have come down to us are only some of a series. He suffered much perplexity and grief because of the conditions in this church. He met Titus in Macedonia on the third missionary journey (he had hoped for him with news from Corinth while he was at Troas). He wrote this letter in response to the messages brought by Titus. He expresses solicitude for them, defends himself against the charges of his enemies, warns them against errors, instructs them in matters of duty and expresses joy that they have heeded his former advice.

Character and Content. It is the least systematic of all Paul's epistles, is full of digressions in subject and difficult of analysis. It is not calm and clear and definite like First Corinthians, but abounds in emotion, showing mingled joy, grief, and indignation. It is intensely personal, telling us of his vision of the third heaven (12:1-4) and of the thorn in the flesh (12:7-9) and many other personal matters so that from it we, therefore, learn more of his life and character than from any other source. This makes it of great value in any study of Paul himself. He clearly hints at at least seven of the charges made against him by his enemies (10:10; 11:6; 2:17; 4:3; 10:8; 5:3). Section one has as its great topic tribulation and consolation in tribulation, and has in it an undercurrent of apology, darkened by a suppressed indignation. Section two is colored by a sorrowful emotion. Section three everywhere teems with a feeling of indignation. Through the whole letter there runs an undercurrent of defense. The "key-note" of this book, as well as of First Corinthians, is loyalty to Christ.

Date. It was written from Macedonia (probably Philippi) in the fall of A. D. 57.

ANALYSIS

Introduction, 1:1-7.

I. Paul's Trials, Principles and Consolations as a Preacher, 1:8-7:16.

1. His interest in the Corinthian church, 1:8-2:11.
2. His service both to God and men, 2:12 end.
3. His appointment by the Holy Spirit, Ch. 3.
4. His power given by God, Ch. 4.
5. His hope of future blessedness, 5:1-19.
6. His exhortation and appeal to the church, 5:20-7:4.
7. His joy at their reception of the word, 7:5 end.

II. The Collection for the Poor Saints, Chs. 8-9.

1. The appeal for liberality, 8:1-15.
2. The sending of Titus and two other brethren, 8:16-9:5.
3. The blessedness of liberality, 9:6 end.

III. Paul's Apostolic Authority, 10:1-13:10.

1. He vindicates his apostolic authority, 10:1-12:13.
2. He warns them that his coming will be with apostolic authority, 12:14-13:10.

Conclusion, 13:11 end.

FOR STUDY AND DISCUSSION

(1) Paul's reasons for not going to Corinth, 1:15-2:4. (2) The glory of the gospel ministry, 4:1-6. (3) His affectionate injunction, 6:11-18. (4) The grace of liberality,

chaps. 8 and 9. Make a list of: (a) Ways of cultivating this grace. (b) The blessings it will bring to the possessor, to others and to the whole church. (5) Paul's boasting, 11:16-12:13. (a) Of what things did he boast? (b) When is boasting justifiable? (6) Paul's self-defense—when should we defend ourselves? (7) The vision of the third heaven, 12:1-4. (8) The thorn in the flesh, 12:7-9. (9) The personal attacks on Paul. Note the hints in 2:17, 4:3; 5:3; 10:8; 10:10; 11:6.

CHAPTER XXIV

GALATIANS, EPHESIANS, AND PHILIPPIANS

Lesson 132. The Book of Galatians, including Analysis, Introductory notes and Scripture reading.

Lesson 133. The Book of Ephesians—Analysis, Introductory Discussions and Scripture reading.

Lesson 134. The Book of Philippians—Analysis, Introductory Discussions and Scripture reading.

GALATIANS

The Country. (1) *Politically* it was the Roman province which included Lycaonia, Isauria, and parts of Phrygia and Pisidia. (2) *Geographically* it was the center of the Celtic tribes, and in this sense it seems to be used in this epistle and in Acts (Gal. 1:2; Acts 13:14; 14:6; 16:6).

The Celtic People. They were descended from the Gauls who sacked Rome in the fourth century B. C., and in the third century B. C. invaded Asia Minor and northern Greece. A part of them remained in Galatia, predominating in the mixed population formed out of the Greek, Roman, and Jewish people. They were quick-tempered, impulsive, hospitable, and fickle people. They were quick to receive impressions and equally quick to give them up. They received Paul with enthusiastic joy, and were then suddenly turned from him (Gal. 4:13-16).

The Churches of Galatia. Just how and by whom these churches were established we do not know. The great highway from the east to Europe passed through this region, making it possible for some of those present at Pentecost to have sown the seed of the gospel there. They could have sprung up from the work done by Paul while at Tarsus from the time of his return from Arabia to his going to Antioch with Barnabas. But the Scripture gives us no word about this.

On the second missionary journey Paul visited them (Acts 16:6) and seems to have taken sick while passing through and to have preached to them while unable to travel (Gal. 4:14-15). They gladly received his teaching, and churches seem to have sprung up. Paul also visited them while on the third missionary journey (Acts 18:23) and instructed and established them in the faith. The churches were running well when Paul left them, but Judaizing teachers had now come in and, acting upon their fickle and unstable nature, had greatly corrupted the simplicity of their faith.

Occasion for the Epistle. (1) Judaizing teachers had gone among the Galatians, claiming that the Jewish law was binding upon Christians, admitting that Jesus was the Messiah, but claiming that salvation must, nevertheless, be obtained by the works of the law. They especially urged that all Gentiles be circumcised. (2) In order to gain their point and turn the Galatians from their belief, they were trying to weaken their confidence in Paul, their spiritual teacher. They said he was not one of the twelve, and therefore not one of the apostles, and his teaching was not of binding authority. They suggested that he had learned his doctrine from others, especially from the apostles who were pillars of the church.

Purpose of the Epistle. The purpose of the epistle was to root out the errors of doctrine introduced by the Judaizers and to hold the Galatians to their earlier faith. To do this it was necessary to establish his apostolic authority and the divine origin of his gospel. He also desired to show the practical value or application of his teaching. He especially shows the value of Christian freedom and at the same time shows that it is not license. In fulfilling these purposes he gave us an inspired classic upon the fundamental doctrine of justification by faith, and forever settled the disturbing question of the relation of Christians to the Jewish law.

Author and Date. It was written by Paul, probably from Corinth, in A. D. 57.

ANALYSIS

Introduction, 1:1-10.

I. Authoritativeness of Paul's Gospel, 1:11-2 end.

1. It is independent of man, 1:11 end.
2. It is the gospel of an apostle, Ch. 2.

II. Teaching of Paul's Gospel, Chs. 3-4. Justification by faith.

1. Their experience proves it, 3:1-5.
2. The example of Abraham attests it, 3:6-9.
3. The scripture teaches it, 3:10-12.
4. The work of Christ provides for it, 3:13-14.
5. Its superior results demonstrate it, 3:15-4:20.
6. The experiences of Sarah and Hagar and their sons illustrate it, 4:21 end.

III. Application of Paul's Gospel to Faith and Conduct, 5:1-6:10.

1. He exhorts them to stand fast in the liberty of Christ, 5:1-12. This liberty excludes Judaism.
2. He exhorts them not to abuse their liberty, 5:13-6:10.

Conclusion, 6:11 end.

FOR STUDY AND DISCUSSION

(1) The dangers of fickleness (1:6; 4:9; 15-16). (2) The methods of false teachers: (a) Their chief method is to attack men prominent in the movement. (b) They usually put forward some one else for leader. They would supplant Paul with Peter. (c) One may well consider how a

man will often allow the influence of another to be undermined if he is himself exalted. (3) The reasons Paul gives to show that his teaching is not of man, 1:11 end. (4) The confirmation of Paul's divine call, 2:1-10. (5) Difference between one under law and under faith, 4:1-7. (6) The lusts of the flesh, sins of body and mind are included, 5:19-21. (7) The fruits of the spirit, 5:22-23. (8) The words, liberty, lust, flesh, spirit, works of the law, live and die, servant and bondage, justified, righteousness, faith and believe. (9) For more advanced study list and study passages in Galatians that coincide with or correspond to passages in Romans.

EPHESIANS

The City. It was the capital of pro-consular Asia, being about a mile from the sea coast, and was the great religious, commercial and political center of Asia. It was noteworthy because of two notable structures there. First, the great theatre which had a seating capacity of 50,000 people, and second, the temple of Diana, which was one of the seven wonders of the ancient world. It was 342 feet long and 164 feet wide, made of shining marble, supported by a forest of columns 56 feet high, and was 220 years in building. This made it the center of the influence of Diana worship, of which we read in Acts 19:23-41. The statue with its many breasts betokened the fertility of nature.

Next to Rome, Ephesus was the most important city visited by Paul. It has been called the third capital of Christianity, it being the center of work in Asia through which were founded all the churches of Asia, especially the seven churches of Asia to which Jesus sent the messages of Revelation. Jerusalem, the birth place of power, is the first, and Antioch, the center of mission work, is the second capital.

Paul's Work at Ephesus. (1) He visited there on the return from the second missionary journey (Acts 18:18-21), and left with them Aquila and Priscilla. (2) On the third missionary journey he spent about three years there (Acts 20-31. (3) During this second visit he had influence enough to check the worship of Diana to such an extent as to arouse the opposition of her worshippers and make it necessary for him to depart into Macedonia (Acts 20:1). (4) On the return from the third missionary journey he stopped at Miletus, thirty miles away, and sent for the elders of Ephesus to whom he delivered a farewell address (Acts 20:16-38).

The Epistle. The contents are much akin to those of Colossians, but also differ greatly from them. (1) In each book half is doctrinal and half practical. (2) Colossians discusses Christ-hood or Christ the head of the church, while Ephesians the ascended Christ is seen in His church. (4) In of Christ. (3) In Colossians Christ is "All and in all," in Ephesians the ascended Christ is seen in His church. (4) In Colossians we have Paul in the heated arena of controversy; in Ephesians he is quietly meditating upon a great theme.

It has been said to contain the profoundest truth revealed to men, and the church at Ephesus was, perhaps, better prepared than any other to be the custodian of such truth, since Paul's long stay there had so well prepared them to hear and understand it. Its thought transcends all local and transitional questions and points to a triumphant universal church of the future. It may have been written as a circular letter to be sent in turn to several churches of which the church at Ephesus was one.

Date. By Paul, probably from Rome, A. D. 62 or 63.

Theme. The church, Christ's mystical body.

ANALYSIS

Salutation, 1:1-2.

I. The Spiritual Blessings of the Church, 1:3-14.

1. The origin of these blessings, v. 3.
2. The blessings enumerated, 4-14.

II. Prayer for the Readers, 1:15 end.

1. That God may grant them the spirit of wisdom, the Holy Spirit, 15-17.
2. That they may know what they have in Christ, 18-23.

III. The Great Work Done for Them, Ch. 2. Both Jews and Gentiles.

1. They were regenerated, 1:10.
2. They were organized, 11 end.

IV. Paul's Mission and Prayer for Them, Ch. 3.

1. His mission to preach the mystery of Christ, 1-13.
2. His prayer for them and doxology of praise to God, 14 end.

V. The Duty of the Church as the Body of Christ, 4:1-6:20.

1. Duty of individual members in relation to other members and the world, 4:1-5:21.
2. Duties of individuals in their home relations, 5:22-6:9.
3. Duties of individual members in their relation to the organized efforts of the church, 6:10-20.

Conclusion, 6:21 end.

FOR STUDY AND DISCUSSION

(1) The Christian's standing before God, Chaps. 1-2. Such words as sealed, chosen, quickened. (2) The blessings of the church, make a list, 1:3-14. (3) The elements and characteristics of the new life, 4:25-32. (4) The different things done in an intelligent Christian life, 5:3-17. (5) The exalted nature and office of Christ, 1:2-23; 2:13-22. (6) The eternal purpose of God, 2:3-5; 3:4-7; 3:9-12. (7) Principles of Christian sociology seen in the home relations such as husband and wife, child and parents, and servant and master. (8) The Christian's relation to Christ as seen in these relations.

PHILIPPIANS

The City. It belonged to Thrace until 358 B. C., when it was seized by Philip, King of Macedonia, father of Alexander the Great. It was the place where Marcus Antonius and Octavius defeated Brutus and Cassius (42 B. C.), which defeat overthrew the Roman Oligarchy, and Augustus (Octavius) was made Emperor. Of the destruction of the city we have no knowledge. There are many ruins there but no systematic excavations have been carried out, and it is uninhabited now. It was on the great highway through which all trade and traders going eastward and westward must pass, and was, therefore, a fit center of evangelism for all Europe. It was the place where the first church of Europe was established by Paul on his second missionary journey, A. D. 52. It was well watered, surrounded by a very fertile territory and adjacent to very rich gold mines.

Paul's Connection with the Church. By a vision from God he went to Philippi on the second missionary journey (Acts 16:9-12). He first preached at a woman's prayer-meeting, where Lydia was converted. She furnished him a home while he continued his work in the city. After some time there arose great opposition to him and he and Silas were beaten and put in prison, but through prayer they were released by an earthquake which also resulted in the conversion of the jailer (Acts, Ch. 16). He perhaps visited them again on his journey from Ephesus to Macedonia (Acts 20:1; II Cor. 2:12-13; 7:5-6). He spent the passover there (Acts 20:6) and received messages from them (Phil. 4:16). They also sent him assistance (Phil. 4:18) and he wrote them this letter.

Character and Purpose of the Letter. It is an informal letter with no logical plan or doctrinal arguments. It is the spontaneous utterance of love and gratitude. It is a tender, warm-hearted, loving friend and brother presenting the essential truths of the gospel in terms of friendly intercourse. He found in them constant reasons for rejoicing, and now that Epaphroditus, who had brought their aid to him, was about to return from Rome to Philippi, he had an opportunity to send them a letter of thanks (Phil. 4:18). It is remarkable for its tenderness, warnings, entreaties and exhortations, and should be read often as a spiritual tonic.

Date. It was written by Paul during his imprisonment at Rome, about A. D. 62.

ANALYSIS

Introduction, 1:1-11.

I. Paul's Present Situation and Feeling, 1:12-26.

II. Some Exhortations, 1:27-2:18.

III. He Plans to Communicate with Them, 2:19 end.

IV. Some Warnings, Ch. 3.

1. Against Judaizers, 1-16.
2. Against false professors, 17 end.

V. Final Exhortation, 4:1-9.

VI. Gratitude for Their Gifts, 4:10-19.

Conclusions, 4:20 end.

FOR STUDY AND DISCUSSION

(1) Paul as a good minister, 1:3-8. (2) Paul's prayer for the Philippians, 1:9-11. (3) The choice between life and death, 1:19-26. (4) Humble-mindedness and its rewards as seen in Jesus, 2:5-11. (5) An upright Christian life, 2:12-18. (6) Paul's sense of imperfection, 3:12-16. (7) Worthy meditations, 4:8-9. (8) Outline the information the book gives concerning Paul's condition at the time of the writing. (9) Point out all the teachings of the book on the necessity of cultivating unselfishness and the blessing derived from it. (10) The expression of joy and rejoicing. (1) The number of times our Lord, under different names, is referred to.

CHAPTER XXV

COLOSSIANS, FIRST AND SECOND THESSALONIANS

Lesson 135. The Book of Colossians, Analysis, Introductory Discussions and Scripture reading.

Lesson 136. First Thessalonians, Scripture reading and everything in these discussions.

Lesson 137. Second Thessalonians and review of all the books from Galatians to II Thessalonians, inclusive.

COLOSSIANS

The City. It was situated about 100 miles east of Ephesus, and was of little importance at the time of this epistle, though it had once been of considerable influence. It was one of a group of three cities, Laodicea and Hierapolis being the other two, situated on the Lycus river near where it flows into the famous Meander. It was on the great highway from Ephesus and the Euphrates Valley. It was the home of many Jews. The place is now called Chonas.

The Church of Colossae. It was perhaps founded by Epaphras (1:6-7; 4:12-13), who was directed by Paul in his work there "for us," "on our behalf," (1:7). Paul, though having a very vital connection with it, had never visited the church (1:7—2:1). He seems to have kept informed about conditions in the church (1:3, 4, 9; 2:1), and to have approved the work and discipline of the church (1:5-7, 23; 2:5-7; 4:12-13). He was loved by them (1:8) and knew and loved some of them. See also Philemon 9.

Condition of the Church and Occasion for the Epistle. False teachers, or a false teacher, had come among them and had greatly hindered the prosperity of the church. The main source of all their false teaching lay in an old eastern dogma, that all matter is evil and its source also evil. If this were true, God, who is in no wise evil, could not have created matter. And since our bodies are matter, they are evil and God could not have created them. From the notion that our bodies are evil three extremes of error arose: (1) That only by various ascetic practices, whereby we punish the body, can we hope to save it, 2:20-23. (2) That since the body is evil, none of its deeds are to be accounted for. License was, therefore, granted to evil conduct, and evil passions were indulged at pleasure and with impunity, 3:5-8. (3) That there could not have been any incarnation of God in the flesh—that deity would not have touched flesh which being matter they regarded as evil.

In seeking to find relief from this condition they formulated two other false doctrines. (1) An esoteric and exclusive theory which was a doctrine of secrets and initiation (2:2, 3, 8). By this doctrine they declared that the remedy for man's condition was known to only a few, and to learn this secret one must be initiated into their company. (2) That since God could not have been creator of these sinful bodies, they could not, therefore, come to Him for blessing, and so they formulated, in their theory, a series of intermediary beings or Aeons, such as angels, that must have created us and whom we must worship (2:18), especially as a means of finally reaching God.

All these false theories conspired to limit the greatness and authority of Jesus Christ, and to limit the sufficiency of redemption in Him (2:9-10). They are called by the one name, Gnosticism, and present four aspects of error in this book. (1) Philosophic, 2:3, 4, 8. (2) Ritualistic, or Judaistic, 2:11, 14, 16-17. (3) Visionary, or angel-worship, 2:18. (4) Ascetic practices, 2:20-23.

There are three modern applications for the Colossian heresy: (1) Ceremonialism, or ritualism, seen in Catholics, etc. (2) Speculation, as seen in Christian Science. (3) Low standards of righteousness, as seen in modern Holiness or Sanctification movements.

The Epistle. The news of these false teachings was brought to Paul probably by Epaphras, 1:7-8, and he wrote to combat them. It is polemic in spirit, and argues that we have everything in Christ, that He is the source and Lord of all creation and that He alone can forgive sins and reconcile us to God. It, therefore, represents more fully than any other of Paul's epistles his doctrine of the person and pre-eminence of Christ.

ANALYSIS

I. **Doctrinal Teachings,** Ch. 1.
  1. Introduction, verses 1-14.
  2. Christ in relation to creation, 15-17.
  3. Christ in relation to the church, 18 end.

II. **Polemic Against False Teachings,** Ch. 2.
  1. Introduction, verses 1-7.
  2. Polemic against the general false teachings, 8-15.
  3. Polemic against the particular claims of the false teachers 16 end.

III. **Hortatory Section,** 3:1-4:16.
  1. To a lofty Christian life, 3:1-4.
  2. To exchange the old vices for the Christian graces, 3:5-14.
  3. To make Christ sovereign over the whole of life, 3:15-17.
  4. To the Christian discharge of relative duties, 3:18-4:1.
  5. To a proper prayer life, 4:2-6.

IV. **Personal Section,** 4:7 end.

FOR STUDY AND DISCUSSION

(1) Paul's prayer for them, 1:9-14. (2) The pre-eminence of the Savior, 1:15-20. (3) The false and true philosophy of religion, 2:8-15. (4) The worldly vices, 3:5-8. (5) The Christian graces, 3:9-14. (6) The lofty Christian

life, 3:15-17. (7) All references to the false teachings as in the words mystery, head, body, Lord, fullness, etc. Note 2:3, 8, 11, 16, 18, and many others. (8) Paul's view of Jesus. Study every reference to Him.

FIRST THESSALONIANS

The City of Thessalonica. It was founded by Cassander, King of Macedon, 315 B. C., and was about a hundred miles west of Philippi. It was a great commercial center of Paul's time, the inhabitants being Greeks, Romans, and Jews. It is located on the Aegean Sea at the head of the Gulf of Salonika, and has remained one of the chief cities of Macedonia from the Hellenistic time down to the present. For centuries it remained one of the chief strongholds of Christianity, and was called the "Orthodox City." From the year 398 A. D., when it was the scene of the great massacre by Theodosius, to 1430 A. D. when the Turks took it, it suffered many massacres and defeats. It still exists under the name of Salonika, and has a population of from 75,000 to 85,000, about half of whom are Jews.

The Church at Thessalonica. Upon being delivered from prison at Philippi, Paul continued his second missionary journey to Thessalonica, having also Silas and Timothy with him (Acts 17:1-5). He spent three Sabbaths there. but on account of the persecution of the Jews, went from there to Berea, then to Athens, and then to Corinth, where he spent 18 months. The first letter bears testimony to the splendid Christian character of these new converts from heathenism. They are an example to others (1:7), their faith had sounded abroad (1:8), they had displayed genuine brotherly love (4:9-10), and a spirit of patience (1:3), joy (1:6), and long-suffering (2:4).

First Thessalonians. This is probably the first epistle written by Paul and perhaps the first written document of the Christian religion. It is not doctrinal, has no element of controversy, and is one of the most gentle and affectionate of Paul's letters. It is notable for its special salutations and refers to their expectations of the immediate return of Jesus. Its main idea is *consolation* (4:17-18), its keynote *hope* and its leading words *affliction* and *advent.* Its purpose was: (1) To send affectionate greetings, (2) to console them in their afflictions, (3) to correct their wrong, their mistaken views of Christ's second coming, (4) to exhort them to proper living as against certain immoral tendencies.

Date. From Corinth A. D. 53.

ANALYSIS

I. The Spiritual Condition of the Church, Ch. 1.

1. Introduction, verse 1.
2. Their faith, love and hope, 2-3.
3. The cause of these, 4-5.
4. The result of these, 6-10.

II. Paul's Character and Conduct While With Them, 2:1-16.

1. How he brought them the gospel, verses 1-12.
2. How they received it, 13-16.

III. Paul's Interest in the Church Since Leaving Them, 2:17-3 end.

1. Desired to visit them, 2:17 end.
2. He sent Timothy to them and rejoiced in his report of them, 3:1-10.
3. Benediction upon them, 3:11 end.

IV. Exhortation for the Future, 4:1-5:11.

1. To purity, 4:1-8.
2. To brotherly love, 4:9-10.
3. To honest industry, 4:11-12.
4. To be comforted in the loss of their dead in Christ, 4:13-5:11.

Conclusion, 5:12.

FOR STUDY AND DISCUSSION

(1) Things in the church for which Paul is thankful. 1:2-6. (2) The different things said about how the gospel was preached to them, 2:1-16. (3) Paul's longing to know about them, 3:1-9. (4) The duties enjoined, 4:1-12. (5) The second coming of Christ and the resurrection, 4:13-18. (6) How we are prepared for the great day of His coming, 5:3-10. (7) The several exhortations in 5:12-22. (8) The human elements or explanations of Paul's power as a preacher, Ch. 2. (9) The deity of Jesus seen in the book.

SECOND THESSALONIANS

This letter was also written from Corinth and during the same year as First Thessalonians, A. D. 53. It is the shortest letter Paul wrote to any church, and is characterized by its lack of special salutations and for its general idea of patient waiting for our Lord. The occasion seems to be to correct their wrong views of the second coming of Christ and the errors of life growing out of these views. It may be that they had misunderstood his own teaching to be that the day of the Lord was already at hand (2:2). At any rate, they believed that He was coming at once, and many of them had quit work and were idly or curiously looking for Him. With all the rest there grew up an evil system that was very bad. Paul saw this and gave directions concerning church discipline (3:6, 14, 15) and idleness (3:12). There is a strong teaching as to the value of courage, calmness, and industry.

ANALYSIS

Introduction, 1:1-2.

I. Thanksgiving and Prayer for Them in View of the Second Coming of Christ, 1:3 end.

II. Warnings About Christ's Second Coming, 2:1-12.

III. Their Escape at His Coming, 2:13 end.

IV. Practical Matters, 3:1-15.

1. **Their prayers for each other, verses 1-5.**
2. **Discipline for the disorderly, 6-15.**

Conclusions, 3:16 end.

FOR STUDY AND DISCUSSION

(1) Things commendable in the church, 1:3-4. (2) Moral disorders of the church, 3:7-11. (3) How to deal with the disorderly, 3:6, 14, 15. (4) How to deal with the idle, 3:12. (5) Facts concerning Christ's second coming, from the whole book. (6) Facts concerning the judgment of the wicked.

CHAPTER XXVI

FIRST AND SECOND TIMOTHY, TITUS, AND PHILEMON

Lesson 138. First Timothy, Scripture and contents of text.
Lesson 139. Second Timothy, Scripture and contents of text.
Lesson 140. Titus and Philemon, Scripture and contents of text

FIRST TIMOTHY

Timothy. He was a native of Lycaonia. His father was a Greek, but his mother and grandmother were Jews, II Tim. 1:5. He was taught the Scriptures from his very youth, II Tim. 3:15, and was probably converted during Paul's first visit to Lystra, Acts 14:8-20. He was ordained as an evangelist, I Tim. 4:14; II Tim. 1:6, and, after Paul's second visit to Lystra, he spent most of his time with Paul, Acts 16:1. He did much valuable service for Paul, and was greatly esteemed by him, Acts 17:14; 18:5, 20:4; Rom. 16:21; I Cor. 4:17; 16:10. His name is associated with Paul in writing a number of letters, II Cor. 1:1; Phil, 1:1; Col. 1:1. He was pastor at Ephesus, and while there received these letters, I Tim. 1:3-4. Paul desired to have him with him when death came, II Tim. 4:9, 13, 21.

The First Epistle to Timothy. This was written while Timothy was pastor at Ephesus, probably between A. D. 64 and 66. Its purpose was to instruct Timothy with regard to his pastoral duties. It, therefore, reflects the condition of the church and especially the errors which he would correct or against which he wished to warn his "true child in the faith." It gives warning against legalistic tendencies and unwise speculations (1:3-11; 4:1-5; 6:20-21), and urges

Timothy to live a spotless life (5:21-22; 4:2; 6:11-16). He indicates a type of men that should be given office in the church (3:1-13), and gives instruction about church government and worship (2:1-2, 8; 3:14-15). It is of much value in showing us the duties of a pastor and the relations he should sustain to the church and to the world.

ANALYSIS

Greetings, 1:1-2.

I. The True Teachings of the Gospel, 1:3 end.

1. Gnostic teachings and the true purpose of the law, 3-11.
2. Paul's salvation, 12-17.
3. Further warnings against false teachers, 18 end.

II. Public Worship, Ch. 2.

1. Prayer, 1-7.
2. Conduct of men and women in church assemblies, 8 end.

III. Church Officers, Ch. 3.

1. A bishop or pastor, 1-7.
2. Deacons and deaconesses, 8-13.
3. A personal word, 14 end.

IV. Pastoral Duties, 4:1-6:2.

1. As to the true doctrine, Ch. 4.
2. Toward the various classes of the church, 5:1-20.
3. Concerning himself, 5:21 end.
4. In teaching slaves and their masters, 6:1-2.

V. Final Warning and Exhortations, 6:3 end.

1. Against false teachers, 3-10.
2. To be truly godly, 11-16.
3. To teach the rich aright, 17-19.
4. To be true to his charge, 20 end.

FOR STUDY AND DISCUSSION

(1) False teaching, 1:3-11; 4:1-8; 6:20-21. (2) The kind of man a pastor should be, 4:12—5:2. (3) The kind of men

to select for church officers, 3:1-13. (Fifteen qualifications of a pastor and seven of a deacon). (4) Church government and services of worship, 2:1, 2, 8; 3:14, 15. (5) The words doctrine or teaching, godliness and faith meaning doctrine.

SECOND TIMOTHY

This letter was written from Rome just before his martyrdom, A. D. 67. It was written to further instruct Timothy and to explain his own personal affairs. It is the last letter written by Paul, a sort of last will and testament, and is of great importance, as it tells us how he fared just before his death. It is more personal in tone than First Timothy, and shows us how very pitiable was his plight in his last days. He longs to see Timothy once more and urges him to "Do your utmost to come unto me soon." In case he does not get there in time, Paul counsels him to be courageous and active in the work (1:6, 7; 2:4-6), and warns him of the evil times that are to come, 3:1-7. As for his own situation all of his companions except Luke have deserted him. He is now in a cold damp dungeon and sighs for his cloak (4:13), and for companionship (4:9, 21). In it all he faces death with triumph.

ANALYSIS

Introduction, 1:1-5.

I. Exhortation to Timothy, 1:6-2 end.

1. To steadfastness in the gospel, 1:6 end.
2. To patient endurance of suffering, 2:1-13.
3. To faithfulness as a pastor, 2:14-26 end.

II. Warnings to Timothy, 3:1-4:5.

1. Concerning the perilous times to come, 3:1-13.
2. Concerning his duties in such times, 3:14-4:5.

III. Paul's View of Death, 4:6-18.

1. His satisfaction and hope at its approach, 6-8.
2. His hope during his loneliness and need, 9-18.

Conclusion, 4:19 end.

FOR STUDY AND DISCUSSION

(1) Paul's condition when he wrote, 1:7, 4:7-18. (2) The desire or appeal of 1:4; 4:5, 9, 13, 21. (3) The exhortation to Timothy 1:6, 7, 13, 14; 2:1-6, 15, 23; 3:14; 4:5. (4) The perilous times to come, Ch. 3. (5) Paul's view of death, 4:5-22.

TITUS

Titus. We do not know much of the work of Titus. But from Gal. 2:1-5; II Cor. 2:12-13; 7:2-16, and Titus 1:5 and 3:12 we learn: (1) That he was a Gentile whom Paul carried to Jerusalem; (2) that by the liberty of the gospel the Jerusalem council did not require him to be circumcised; (3) that he was a capable and energetic missionary; (4) that Paul had left him in Crete to finish the work which he had begun there.

The Book. The book is written to counsel Titus concerning the work Paul had left him to do (1:5). It contains: (1) the qualifications of the presbyters to be selected; (2) the method of dealing with false teachings and the importance of sound doctrine; (3) instructions to the different classes of the church, including the young, the aged, and slaves; (4) exhortations to Titus himself, in which he urges him to be an example of good works, 12:7-8.

Date. Probably written from Macedonia, A. D. 66.

ANALYSIS

Greeting, 1:1-4.

I. Qualifications and Duties of Bishops or Pastors, 1:5 end.

1. **The qualifications and duties, 5-9.**
2. **Reasons for needing such officers, 10 end.**

II. Instruction in Practical Godliness, 2:1-3:11.

1. **Proper conduct for the different classes and its basis, Ch. 2.**
2. **Proper conduct in the different life relations, 3:1-11.**

Conclusion, 3:12-15.

FOR STUDY AND DISCUSSION

In the first two topics lists should be made; in the other four what is said about the word in each place where it is mentioned should be considered. (1) The qualifications of presbyters, 1:5-10. (2) The lofty moral ideas for all Christians, 2:1-15. (3) *Savior* and *salvation,* used seven times (1:3; 2:10, 11, 13; 3:4, 5, 6). (4) *Good works* or *good things,* the key-word of the epistle, used seven times (1:16; 2:7, 14; 3:1, 8, 14). *Sound doctrine* occurs seven times in this form or as sound in the faith, incorruption in doctrine, sound speech or doctrine of God (1:9, 13; 2:1, 7, 8, 10). (6) *Sober-minded* occurring six times, at least in thought (1:8; 2:2, 4, 6, 12). These last three constitute the apostle's idea of real godliness.

PHILEMON

Philemon lived at Colossae and was probably a convert of Paul and a member of the Colossian church. Onesimus was a slave of Philemon who had robbed his master (18) and fled to Rome, where he had been converted under Paul's preaching (10). It is the only individual or private letter written by Paul, and is written to tell Philemon of the conversion of Onesimus and to make a plea for him. Through the kindness shown Onesimus we have revealed to us the great kindness of the apostle's heart. He speaks to Philemon not as an apostle in authority, but as a friend to a friend, thereby showing his great courtesy. The letter is of inestimable value as showing the power of the gospel to win and transform a poor slave and to soften the harsh relations between the different classes of ancient society.

Its teachings are such as to forever overthrow all slavery of human beings.

Date. From Rome about A .D. 63.

ANALYSIS

1. Introduction, 1-7.
2. The purpose of the letter—an appeal to Onesimus, 8-21.
3. Closing matters, 22 end.

FOR STUDY AND DISCUSSION

(1) How Christianity deals with slaves. (2) The effectiveness of the Christian religion in a life. (a) Even a fugitive slave would confess his guilt, as, no doubt, Onesimus had done to Paul. (b) It will make one desire to correct any wrongs one has done, and willing, as was Onesimus, to go to the one wronged and make confession. (c) It often raises one from worthlessness to great usefulness (verse 11). (d) It will not only make one useful to others in temporal matters, but will make one profitable in things spiritual (verse 13). (3) Concerning a real Christian helper, we may learn that, like Paul: (a) He will not try to hide or cover up a man's past faults. (b) He will sympathize with the poor fellow who has a bad record behind him. (c) He will make it as easy as possible for such a convert to right the past. (d) He will gladly use the very humblest Christian (verse 13). (e) He will be courteous and recognize the rights of others, as in the case of Philemon. (f) He will not force a man to do his duty, but he will use love and persuasion to bring him to it. (4) Make a list of all the persons named and learn something of each.

CHAPTER XXVII

HEBREWS AND JAMES

Lesson 141. **Analysis, Introductory Discussions and Chs. 1-5 of Hebrews.**

Lesson 142. **Hebrews, Chs. 6-13.**

Lesson 143. **The book of James—Scripture reading and content of the text.**

HEBREWS

The Author. The author nowhere indicates his name, and there is difference of opinion as to who wrote it. I am personally inclined to the view of those who regard Paul as the author, which for a long time was the common view. The main points against his authorship are that the language and style are dissimilar to Paul's and that it is less like an epistle than any other book that bears his name. It seems clear, however, that the thoughts and course of reasoning are Pauline and that the differences otherwise may be explained by the difference of purpose and spirit in writing. For the arguments for and against his authorship the student is referred to the larger commentaries and introductions to the New Testament literature.

Those to Whom It Was Written. It was, no doubt, addressed to Hebrew Christians, but whether to a special church or to those in a special locality, is a matter of dispute. Several things, however, may be learned about them. (1) They had steadfastly endured persecution and the loss of property. (2) They had showed sympathy with other Christians, 6:10; 10:32-34. (3) They had been

Christians some time, 5:12. (4) They knew the writer who asked that by their prayers they should help restore him to themselves, 13:18-19. (5) They knew Timothy who was to visit them, 13:23. (6) They were now in danger of apostasy to Judaism, but had not yet resisted to blood, 12:3-4.

Their danger of going back to Judaism might arise from several sources. (1) There was a tendency to disbelieve Christ and His claims, 3:12. (2) The elaborate worship of the temple compared with the simple worship of the Christian church. (3) The Jews branded them as traitors and taunted them for turning against the law, which was given by prophets, angels, and Moses, and from the sanctuary ministered to by the priests of God. (4) They were suffering persecution.

Purpose and Contents. The purpose was to prevent apostasy from Christianity to Judaism and incidentally to comfort them in their suffering and persecution. To accomplish this purpose the author shows, by a series of comparisons, that the religion of Christ is superior to that which preceded it. "Better" is the key-word, which along with other terms of comparison, such as "more excellent," is constantly used to show the superiority of Christianity. Special emphasis is put on Christ as our High Priest before God. In it all there are many solemn warnings and earnest exhortations. It is very much like a sermon, the author often turning aside to exhort, then returning to the theme.

Date. It was written from Jerusalem, Alexandria or Rome some time before A. D. 70, since the temple was still standing, 9:6-8; 10:1.

Theme. Christianity superior to Judaism.

ANALYSIS

I. Christianity Is Superior to Judaism Because Christ Through Whom It Was Introduced Is Superior to the Messengers of Judaism, Chs. 1-6.

1. He is superior to prophets, 1:1-3.
2. He is superior to angels, 1:4-2 end.
3. He is superior to Moses, including Joshua, Chs. 3-6.

Three points in each of these comparisons are the same:

1. He is God's Son.
2. He is man's Savior.
3. He is man's high priest.

Neither prophets nor angels nor Moses equal Jesus in these points.

There are two notable exhortations, (a) 2:1-4; (b) 5:11-6 end.

II. Christianity Is Superior to Judaism Because Its Priesthood Is Superior to That of Judaism, 7:1-10:18.

1. Christ its priest is superior to the priests of Judaism, 7:1-8:6.
2. Its covenant is superior to that of Judaism, 8:7 end.
3. Its tabernacle is superior to that of Judaism, 10:1-18.

III. Christianity Is Superior to Judaism, Because the Blessings It Confers Are Superior to Those of Judaism, 10:19-12 end.

1. In the liberty of approach to God, 10:19 end.
2. In the superior ground in faith, 11:1-12:17.
3. In our coming to Mount Zion instead of Mount Sinai, 12:18 end.

IV. Practical Conclusions, Ch. 13.

FOR STUDY AND DISCUSSION

(1) Description of Christ, 1:1-3. (2) Christ's superiority to angels, 1:3-14. (3) Christ's humiliation for our salvation, 2:9-18. (4) How is Christ superior to Aaronic priests, 4:14, 15; 5:1-7, 9; 7:28. (5) The two covenants 8:6-12. (6) Typical character of the old ordinances, 9:1-10:4. (7) Our assurance and hope, 6:13-20. (8) The danger of rejecting Christ, 10:26-31. (9) The benefit of affliction, 12:4-11. (10) The comparisons of 12:18-29. (11) The warning of 13:9-15. (12) The exhortations of the book, as 2:1-4. (13) Make a list of all the terms of comparison, as better and more excellent. (14) Make a list of every reference to Christ as high priest. (15) Every reference to the Holy Spirit—what are His works and where in the book is it taught?

JAMES

Author. Three persons called James are mentioned in the New Testament. One of these is James, the Lord's brother (Matt. 13:55), who did not believe on Jesus until after the resurrection, Jno. 7:2-9; Mark 3:21, 31; Acts 1:13-14. This James occupied an important place as pastor at Jerusalem, and made an important speech at the council of the Apostles, Acts 15:13-21. He is mentioned elsewhere, in Acts 12:17; Gal. 1:19; 2:9-12. Josephus tells us that he was stoned to death about 62 A. D on a charge of departing from the Jewish law. This James, the Lord's brother, is supposed to be the author of this epistle.

To Whom Written. The letter was written to the Jews scattered everywhere, 1:1, and evidently to Christian Jews, 2:1. Some of them were rich, some poor, 2:1-10. They were lustful, greedy, and proud, 4:1-12, and were omitting to do the Lord's work as they should, 1:22-27.

The Epistle. The chief characteristic of style is abruptness. Change is made from one subject to another with no effort to connect them. There is, therefore, no general subject, and a lack of close connection between the points of analysis. "Faith without works is dead" flashes in every section as a sort of bond of unity. It is eloquent, stern, and sincere, and has a distinct Jewish tone. It lacks the doctrinal emphasis found in Paul and states the Christian faith in terms of moral excellence and instructs them in the subject of Christian morals. It is notable for its omissions. It does not have the word gospel, does not allude to the work of redemption, the incarnation, the resurrection or ascension, and only mentions Christ's name twice. It is calculated to fortify Christians in their trials (1:2; 2:6-7; 5:1-6) and to correct their errors in personal and Church life (1:19-21; 2:14-26; 4:1-5:11; 2:1-9). It has a decided Jewish tone and is closely related to the wisdom books of the Old Testament. It has many allusions to nature and natural objects and reflects the civilization of the time.

Date and Place of Writing. It was no doubt written from Jerusalem where he was a pastor, but the date is much disputed. Some put it as early as A. D. 40. Others, among whom is Dr. Robertson, say it was written not later than A. D. 50. Still others put it about A. D. 61, just before the martyrdom of James. It is probably safe to say that it was one of the very earliest of the New Testament books.

ANALYSIS

Salutation, 1:1.

I. Proper Attitude Towards Trials, 1:2-18.

II. Proper Attitude Towards God's Word, 1:19-27 end.

III. Various Warnings, 2:1-4:12.

1. Against respect of persons, 2:1-13.
2. Against barren professions of faith, 2:14-26.
3. Against the dangers of the tongue, 3:1-12.
4. Against false wisdom, 3:13-18.
5. Against quarrels, greed and pride, 4:1-12.

IV. Various Denunciations, 4:13-5:6.

V. Various Exhortations, 5:7-20 end.

FOR STUDY AND DISCUSSION

(1) From the following scriptures make a list of all the things James advises us not to do: 1:6, 13, 16, 22; 2:1, 14; 3:1, 10; 4:1, 11, 13; 5:9, 12. (2) From the following scriptures make a list of all the things James advises us to do: 1:2, 4, 5, 6, 9, 11, 22, 26; 2:8, 12, 3:13; 4:8; 5:7, 10, 12, 13, 16. (3) Make a sketch of heavenly wisdom, showing the different things said about it, studying especially, 1:5-8 and 3:13-18. (4) Study the ethics of speech and of the tongue, 1:19-21 and 3:1-12. (5) Life's trials and temptations, 1:2-4, 12-15. (6) Make a list of all the figures of speech, especially similes and metaphors, as "a doubter is like a surge of the sea," 1:6. (7) James' rebuke of selfishness, 5:1-6. (8) The utility and power of prayer, 5:13-18.

CHAPTER XXVII

FIRST AND SECOND PETER

Lesson 144. First Peter, Scripture reading and all Discussions and Studies of the text.

Lesson 145. Second Peter, Scripture and text.

FIRST PETER

Author. The author was the Apostle Peter, whose name before he became a disciple, was Simon. He was born in Bethsaida and lived in Capernaum, where he followed the occupation of fishing. He was brought to Jesus by Andrew, his brother, and became one of the leaders of the Apostles, both before and after Christ's death. His career should be studied as it is found in Acts. He was impetuous, brave and energetic, and after the ascension performed many miracles.

Those Addressed. The sojourners of the dispersion (1:1) points to Jewish Christians. They were strangers (sojourners) 1:1, 17; 2:11, who were persecuted, 3:17; 4:12-19, but persecution came, not from the Jews, but from pagans, 4:3-4. They had certain faults and wrong tendencies, 2:1, 11, 12, 16; 3:8-12; 4:9; 5:2-3.

Purpose. To console them in their suffering, and to exhort them to faithfulness and duty, (1:7; 3:17; 4:12). The letter is filled with the spirit of consolation and in all ages has strengthened those who were undergoing trials. It also fortified them against the temptations to which their immoral heathen surroundings subjected them (1:13-16; 2:11-12; 4:1-6). Connected with these teachings are found strong exhortations to purity and holiness of life.

Date. Probably about 64-68 A. D. Certainly not after 70 A. D., as he was no doubt put to death before then.

ANALYSIS

Introduction, 1:1-2.

I. Thanksgiving for the Blessings of Grace, 1:3-12.

1. **For a living hope and an abiding inheritance, 3-5.**
2. **For joyful faith during trials, 6-9.**
3. **For salvation, 10-12.**

II. Obligations Growing Out of the Blessings of Grace, 1:13-4:19.

1. **A right relation of the heart toward God and man, 1:13-2:10.**
2. **Right conduct in life relations, 2:11-3:12.**
3. **Right attitude toward suffering, 3:13-4:19 end.**

III. Exhortations to Particular Classes, 5:1-9.

Conclusion, 5:10 end.

FOR STUDY AND DISCUSSION

(1) Peter's loyalty to Christ. (a) He makes everything depend on Christ, His cross (1:18-19; 2:24; 3:18), His suffering (2:21; 3:18; 4:13), His resurrection (1:3), His manifestation (1:7-13), His exaltation (3:22; 4:11; 5:10). (b) He calls Christ a living stone, 2:4-8. (c) He clings to Christ's teaching, submission to rightful authority (2:13-16), forgiveness of others (4:8; Matt. 18:22), humility (5:5). (2) The mercy of God our hope, 1:3-7. From this passage list what is said of spiritual inheritors and their inheritance. (3) How to obtain the Christian deal, 1:13-21. (4) Spiritual development, 2:1-10. (5) Various duties of society, 2:13-17; of domestic life, 2:18; 3:1, 7; of Christian brotherhood, 1:22; 2:1-5; 3:8-9; 4:8-11; 5:1-5. (6) The work of the different persons of the Trinity. (7) The words precious, joy and rejoicing, mercy, love and faith.

SECOND PETER

Occasion for the Epistle. The occasion for the epistle is found in the harm being done to the church by false teachers, who were of two classes, the libertines and the mockers, against whom he warns them.

Purpose. Its purpose was to exhort them to Christian growth and to warn them against false teachers. This is seen in his warnings against them (2:1-21; 3:3-7, 16).

Comparison with First Peter. It has no reference to Christ's death, suffering, resurrection and ascension. Glance through I Peter again to see how often these are mentioned. The spirit manifested is one of anxiety, severity, sweetness and fatherly dignity. It connects the second coming of Christ with the punishment of the wicked, while I Peter connects it with the glorification of the saints. Its key-note is knowledge, while that of I Peter is hope.

Some Teachings. (1) To be holy, not to secure an inheritance, but because we already have it. (2) To love the brethren, not to purify our soul, but because it is pure. (3) That we sacrifice, not as penance, but as an expression of praise.

ANALYSIS

Introduction, 1:1-2.

I. Progress in the Christian Life, 1:3-21 end.
1. An exhortation to growth, 3-11.
2. Reasons for these exhortations, 12-21.

II. False Teachers, Ch. 2.
1. The evil teachers and their followers, 1-3.
2. Their punishment, 4-10.
3. Their character, evil ways and end, 11-22.

III. The Second Coming of Christ, 3:1-13. He will bring both blessings and destruction.

Conclusion, 3:14-18.

FOR STUDY AND DISCUSSION

(1) What our salvation involves, 1:5-11. (2) The characteristics of the false teachers, 2:1-3, 10, 12-14. (3) The certain punishment of these false teachers, 2:4-6, 15, 16, 21, 22. (4) The exhortations of the book to sobriety, etc., 1:3. (5) The predictions of the book.

CHAPTER XXIX

FIRST, SECOND, AND THIRD JOHN AND JUDE

Lesson 146. First John—Scripture and all Discussions and Studies of the text.

Lesson 147. II and III John and Jude—Scripture and all Discussions and Studies of the text.

FIRST JOHN

Author and Date. It was probably written from Ephesus. 80 or 85 A. D., though some put it as early as A. D. 69, while others put it as late as A. D. 95. The author nowhere indicates his name, but through all the centuries it has been attributed to John, the beloved disciple. For information concerning him see the discussions on the Gospel of John.

Readers. It was doubtless written primarily to the churches of Asia Minor in which John by reason of his work at Ephesus had a special interest. It is evident that those addressed were of all ages and were hated of the world. They were inclined to worldliness and to the danger of looking too lightly upon sin. They were also in danger of being led into doubt by those who denied the deity of Jesus.

Style. It is more in the form of a sermon or pastoral address than of an epistle. It is written with a tone of conscious authority. The thought is profound and mystical, but the language is simple both in words and in sentences. The arguments are by immediate inference. There are many contrasts, parallelisms and repetitions with no figures of speech except perhaps the words light and darkness.

Character and Purpose. The chief purpose was to tell them how they might know that they had eternal life, 5:13. The accomplishment of this purpose would also assure the fulfillment of the secondary purpose stated in 1:3, 4. It is more like a sermon than a letter. He lays special emphasis on a few great truths such as: God is Light (1:5); and those that have fellowship with Him must walk in the light or do deeds of righteousness (1:6-7; 2:9-11; 3:17-23); The love of God for His children (3:1-2; 4:8-11, 16, 19); Christian duty to love one another (2:10; 3:10-24; 4:7-21; 5:1-2); The atoning work of Christ (1:7; 2:1-2; 4:10).

ANALYSIS

Introduction, 1:1-4.

I. **How Those Who Possess Eternal Life Will Live, 1:5-5:12.**

1. They will dwell in the light, 1:5-2:28.
2. They will do righteousness, 2:29-4:6.
3. They will live a life of love, 4:7-5:3.
4. They will walk by faith, 5:4-12.

II. **What Those Who Live Such Lives May Know, 5:13-20.**

1. That they have eternal life, 13.
2. That their prayers are answered, 14-17.
3. That God's people do not live in sin, 18.
4. Their true relation to God and Christ, 19-20.

Conclusion, 5:21.

The following analysis made with the idea of the theme being "Fellowship with God" (1:3-4) is very suggestive:

Introduction, 1:1-4.

I. **God Is Light** and our fellowship with Him depends upon our walking in the light, 1:5-2:28.

II. **God Is Righteous** and our fellowship with Him depends upon our doing righteousness, 2:29-4:6.

III. **God Is Love** and our fellowship with Him depends upon our having and manifesting a spirit of love, 4:7-5:3.

IV. **God Is Faithful** and our fellowship with Him depends upon our exercising faith in Him, 5:4-12.

Conclusion, 5:13-21 end.

FOR STUDY AND DISCUSSION

(1) The different things we may know and how we may know them. Make a list giving reference, as, "know Him if we keep His commandments" (2:3). (2) Make a list of the things defined in the following scriptures, and give the definition in each case: 1:5; 2:25; 3:11; 3:23; 5:3; 5:4; 5:11; 5:14. (3) The several figures and attributes of God, as light, righteousness and love. (4) The requirements of deeds of righteousness, 1:6, 7; 2:9-11; 3: 17-23. (5) God's love for His children, 3:1-2; 4:8-11, 16, 19. (6) Christians' duty to love one another, 2:10; 3:10-24; 4:7-21; 5:1-2.

SECOND JOHN

It is a friendly, personal letter, written some time after the first letter, to the "elect lady" who, as I think, was John's friend, and not a church or some nation as has sometimes been argued. The aim is evidently to warn his friends against certain false teachers who are endangering them.

ANALYSIS

1. Greeting, 1-3.
2. Thanksgiving, 4.
3. Exhortation to obedience, 5-6.
4. Warning against antichrist, 7-9.
5. How to deal with false teachers, 10-11.
6. Conclusion, 12-13.

FOR STUDY AND DISCUSSION

(1) The character of the children of the elect lady. (2) Evidence of real discipleship. (3) How to deal with false teachers.

THIRD JOHN

This also is a private letter written some time after First John, to his personal friend, Gaius. There was some confusion about receiving certain evangelists. Gaius had received them while Diotrephes had opposed their reception. He commends Gaius for his Christian hospitality and character and assures him of the writer's expectation of a visit shortly.

ANALYSIS

1. Greeting, 1.
2. Prayer for his posterity, 2.
3. Commends his godly walk, 3-4.
4. Commends his hospitality, 5-8.
5. Complaint against Diotrephes, 9-10.
6. Test of relation to God, and worth of Demetrius, 11-12.
7. Conclusion, 13-14.

FOR STUDY AND DISCUSSION

(1) The character of Gaius and Diotrephes. (2) Christian hospitality. (3) Such words as truth, sincerity and reality.

JUDE

Author. The author is named Jude, the brother of James. He probably means the James who wrote the epistle of that name and is, therefore, the Lord's brother.

Purpose. False teachers were boldly teaching their heresies in the meetings of the congregation. These men were also very immoral in conduct and the epistle is written to condemn these ungodly men, to expose their errors and to exhort his readers to contend for the true faith and to live worthy lives. In many points it is very similar to the second letter of Peter. It shows something of the extent and seriousness of the difficulties with which the early Christians had to contend.

Date. It was probably written about A. D. 66. At any rate it must have been written before A. D. 70 when Jerusalem was destroyed, as Jude would hardly have failed to mention that event along with other examples of punishment, 5-7.

ANALYSIS

Introduction, 1-4.

I. The Fate of Wicked Disturbers, 5-16.

1. God punishes the wicked, 5-7.
2. He will destroy these men, 8-16.

II. How to Contend for the Faith, 17-23.

1. Be mindful of the enemies, 17-19.
2. Be strong (built up in the faith), 20-21.
3. Maintain an evangelistic spirit, 22-23.

Conclusion, 24-25.

FOR STUDY AND DISCUSSION

(1) Make a list of all the words and phrases occurring in threes, as mercy, love, peace, or Cain, Baalam, Korah. (2) Make a list of all the different things taught about the evil workers mentioned, 8-10, 12, 13, 16, 19. (3) What the apostles had foretold concerning them.

CHAPTER XXX

REVELATION

Lesson 148. **Analysis, Introductory Discussion and Ch. 1-5.**

Lesson 149. **Revelation, Chs. 17-22.**

Lesson 150. **Review—First Timothy to Revelation inclusive.**

Author and Date. The author was John, the apostle. He wrote it while in exile on the Isle of Patmos (1:1, 4, 9; 22:8), about 95 or 96 A. D.

The Book. (1) It is a book of symbols and imagery, and constantly creates excitement and wonder. (2) It is a book of wars, but war always ends in peace. The word war occurs nine times in Revelation, and only seven times in all the rest of the New Testament. (3) It is a book of thunder, but the thunder and earthquake die away and are followed by liturgies and psalms. (4) It is a book of the rewards of the righteous. This is seen in the letters to the seven churches, and in the victories of the right in all conflicts and wars of the book. (5) It is, therefore, a book of optimism. Everywhere God overcomes Satan, the Lamb triumphs, Babylon falls, etc.

Its Interpretation. There are several classes of interpreters, as follows: (1) *The Praeterist,* who thinks it has been filled in its primary sense. He makes all the prophecies and visions refer to Jewish history down to the fall of Jerusalem, and to the history of pagan Rome. (2) *The Futurist,* who interprets literally and thinks all the events of the book are to come just before or just after the second coming of Christ. (3) *The Historical or Continuous School.* these think some have been fulfilled, some are now being fulfilled, and some will be fulfilled in the future. (4) *The Spiritualist,* who objects to the other three classes of interpreters because they make so much of the time element. He lays stress upon the moral and spiritual element of the book and reads the book "as a representation of ideas rather than events."

Value. The chief value of the book seems to lie in its testimony to the faith and hope of persecuted Christians and in the comfort and inspiration it has brought to sorrowing and oppressed souls of every age. It points out that there will be an end of conflict, that God and the Lamb will triumph, that the enemies of our souls will be punished and that the followers of God will be rewarded with eternal reward.

ANALYSIS

Introduction, 1:1-8.

I. **The Seven Churches,** 1:9-3 end.

1. A preparatory vision of Christ, 1:9 end.
2. The addresses to the churches, Chs. 2-3.

II. **The Seven Seals,** 4:1-8:1.

1. A preparatory vision of the throne, Chs. 4-5.
2. Six seals opened in order, Ch. 6.
3. An episode—sealing God's servants, Ch. 7.
4. The seventh seal opened, 8:1.

III. **The Seven Trumpets,** 8:2-11 end.

1. A preparatory vision, 8:2-6.
2. Six trumpets sounded in order, 8:7-9 end.

3. An episode—little book, measuring the temple and two witnesses, 10:1-11:14.
4. The seventh trumpet sounded, 11:15 end.

IV. The Seven Mystic Figures, Chs. 12-14.

1. The sun-clothed woman, Ch. 12.
2. The red dragon, Ch. 12.
3. The man-child, Ch. 12.
4. The beast from the sea, 13:1-10.
5. The beast from the earth, 13:11-18.
6. The Lamb on Mount Zion, 14:1-13.—Three angels
7. The Son of man on the cloud, 14:14-20.—Three angels.

V. The Seven Vials, Chs. 15-16.

1. The preliminary vision, Ch. 15—a song of victory.
2. Six vials poured out in order, 16:1-12.
3. An episode, 16:13-16. The spirits of the devil gathered the kings of the earth to the battle of Armageddon.
4. The seventh vial poured out, 16:17-21 end.

VI. The Final Conflicts and Triumphs, 17:1-22:5.

1. The first conflict and triumph, 17:1-19:10.
2. The second conflict and triumph, 19:11-20:6.
3. The third conflict and triumph, 20:7-22:5.

VII. The Epilogue Conclusion, 22:6-21 end.

1. Threefold testimony to the truth of the vision, Angel, Jesus, John, 6-8.
2. Directions of the angels concerning the prophecy, 9-10.
3. The moral of the book, 11-17.
4. John's attestation and salutation, 18-21.

FOR STUDY AND DISCUSSION

(1) The vision of Jesus, 1:9 end. (2) The letters to the seven churches. (a) Which churches are given nothing but praise? (b) Which nothing but blame? (c) Which both

praise and blame? (d) What is commended and what is condemned in each? (3) The twenty-four elders, four living creatures, sealed book and the Lamb, Chs. 4-5. (4) The sealing of God's servants, Ch. 7. (5) The little book, Ch. 10. (6) The measuring rod and two witnesses, 11:1-14. (7) Each of the seven mystic figures, Chs. 12-14. Describe each. (8) Mystery Babylon, Ch. 17. (9) Song of triumph over Babylon, 19:1-10. (10) The judgment of Satan, 20: 1-10. (11) The description of the general resurrection and judgment, 20:11-15; 22:10-15. (12) The description of heaven, Chs. 21-22. (13) Verify the following points of similarity in the seven seals, seven trumpets, and seven vials: (a) that heaven is opened and a preliminary vision before each series; (b) that the first four in each refer especially to the present natural world, while the last three in each series refer more particularly to the future or spiritual world; (c) that in each series there is an episode after the sixth which is either an elaboration of the sixth or an introduction to the seventh. (14) Compare these three series again and note: (a) that they portray the same events in similar language; (b) that the victory of the righteous and the destruction of the wicked are portrayed in each; (c) that the victory of the redeemed predominates in the first (seals) while the destruction of the wicked predominates in the last (vials). (15) In the series note the progress in the severity of punishment: (a) one-fourth afflicted in the first (seals); (b) one-third afflicted in the second (trumpets); (c) all are destroyed in the third (vials). (16) From the following scriptures make a list showing how nearly the same thing is affected in each of the seven trumpets and vials, (a) 8:7 and 16:2; (b) 8:8 and 16:3; (c) 8:10-11 and 16:4-7; (d) 8: 12 and 16:8-9; (e) 9:9-11 and 16:10-11; (f) 9:13-21 and 16:12-16; (g) 11:15-18 and 16:17-21. (17) The contrasts are resemblances of the trumpets and vials. These may be seen from the following comparisons:

TRUMPETS	VIALS
1. Hail, fire, blood cast on earth, one-third of the trees burned.	1. The vial poured out on the earth, affliction upon the followers of the beast.
2. One-third of the sea made blood, one-third of its creatures and its ships destroyed.	2. The whole sea made blood, and every soul therein destroyed.
3. One-third of the rivers made bitter, many men destroyed.	3. All the rivers made blood and vengeance upon all men.
4. One-fourth of the sun, etc., smitten, one-third of the day darkened.	4. The whole sun smitten men are scorched, they blaspheme and repent not.
5. The stars of heaven fall into the pit; locusts sent forth; men seek death.	5. The throne and kingdom of the beast smitten, men suffer and blaspheme and repent not.
6. One-third of the men destroyed by the armies of the Euphrates; men do not repent.	6. A way prepared for the kings beyond the Euphrates.
Episode: God's two witnesses witness for Him and work miracles. War against them by the beasts.	Episode: The dragon's three unclean spirits witness for him and work miracles. War by the world at Armageddon.
7. Voice in heaven, judgment, earthquakes, hail, etc.	7. Voice in heaven, fall of Babylon, earthquake, hail, etc.

(18) The benedictions and doxologies of the book. (19) Things taught about Jesus. (20) Things taught about Satan.